HUNTER

New
95

The Defiant Muse

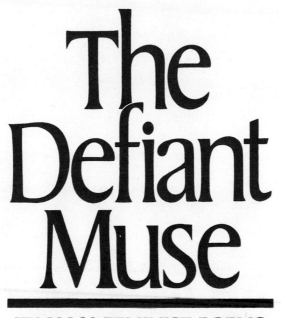

ITALIAN FEMINIST POEMS FROM THE MIDDLE AGES TO THE PRESENT

THE DEFIANT MUSE
Series Editor, Angel Flores

The Defiant Muse: Italian Feminist Poems from the Middle Ages to the Present
Edited by Beverly Allen, Muriel Kittel, and Keala Jane Jewell and with an introduction by Beverly Allen

The Defiant Muse: Hispanic Feminist Poems from the Middle Ages to the Present
Edited and with an introduction by Ángel Flores and Kate Flores

The Defiant Muse: French Feminist Poems from the Middle Ages to the Present
Edited and with an introduction by Domna C. Stanton

The Defiant Muse: German Feminist Poems from the Middle Ages to the Present
Edited and with an introduction by Susan L. Cocalis

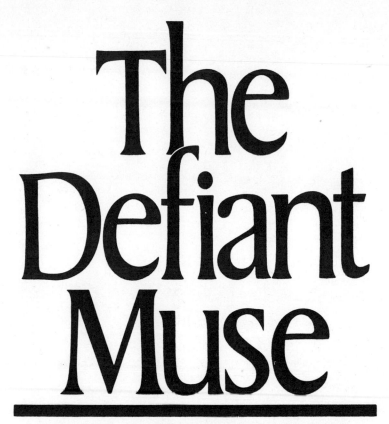

The Defiant Muse

ITALIAN FEMINIST POEMS FROM THE MIDDLE AGES TO THE PRESENT

A BILINGUAL ANTHOLOGY

EDITED BY BEVERLY ALLEN, MURIEL KITTEL
AND KEALA JANE JEWELL

INTRODUCTION BY BEVERLY ALLEN

THE FEMINIST PRESS
AT THE CITY UNIVERSITY OF NEW YORK
NEW YORK

89 88 87 86   6 5 4 3 2 1

Permission acknowledgments begin on page 149.

Cover and text design by Gilda Hannah
Typeset by Weinglas Typography Inc.
Manufactured by Banta Company

This publication is made possible, in part, by public
funds from the New York State Council on the Arts.

All translations by Muriel Kittel, unless otherwise noted.

Library of Congress Cataloging-in-Publication Data
Italian feminist poems from the Middle Ages to
the present.
    (The Defiant muse)
    English and Italian.
    1. Feminist poetry, Italian—Translations into
English. 2. English poetry—Translations from
Italian. 3. Feminist poetry, Italian. I. Allen,
Beverly. II. Kittel, Muriel. III. Jewell, Keala Jane. IV.
Series.
PQ4205.E518 1986   851'.008'09287   86-4841
ISBN 0-935312-48-X
ISBN 0-935312-55-2 (pbk.)

I did not want to sing, I wanted to speak,
and tell about myself, about so many women
whose numerous desires arouse their sleepless
hearts and leave them with slightly bitter lips.

—*Amalia Guglielminetti*

I want so strongly our freedom
in the red round dance of defiance
I want to sing so strongly
that the song could break my heart
and go on living
without me.

—*Franca Maria Catri*

PUBLISHER'S PREFACE

The Feminist Press is proud to publish this set of anthologies of feminist poetry, the first bilingual collection of its kind. When Domna C. Stanton proposed the project to The Press in 1983, I immediately responded that it was "a natural" for The Press, and a critical publication in women's studies that was long overdue. To be sure, the idea for the series and the actual work began years earlier. In 1976, Kate Flores urged Angel, her husband, to collaborate on an anthology, not simply of women's poetry, which had been sporadically included in the more than twenty volumes of verse he had edited, but specifically of feminist poetry, which had never been done. However, as the enormity of the undertaking became apparent, they enlarged the original scope from one to four volumes, each to be devoted to a major language, and contacted Domna C. Stanton for French, Susan L. Cocalis for German, and Beverly Allen and Muriel Kittel for Italian. In common, these editors agreed upon the general conception of the volumes; independently, over a period of several years, they did extensive research in libraries at home and in the countries of origin. That arduous process led to a "re-vision" of poets whose feminism had been ignored or suppressed. Far more important, it led to the discovery of numerous poets whose work remains unknown in their own country to this day. Thanks to these editors, the poetry can now have the audience it deserves.

Reading each volume produces the exciting awareness of a strong national tradition of feminist poetry, dating back to "the dark ages." Together, the anthologies confirm the existence of many common themes and threads that connect women beyond differences of class and culture, time and place. For that inspiring vision, the editors of this series, like those of us at The Feminist Press, can be proud...and joyful.

Florence Howe

The editors extend special thanks to Biancamaria Frabotta for her advice and help with the preparation of the biographical notes, in selecting poems from earlier periods and in suggesting contemporary authors. We are grateful to Vivian Lamarque, Jolanda Insana, and Gabriela Sica for sending us copies of their work. We gratefully remember the late Laura Di Nola for poems from *Poesia femminista italiana*. We thank Biancamaria Frabotta for poems from *Donne in poesia* and G. M. Loperfido for poems from *Versi d'amore*. Some valuable biographical material was found in Natalia Costa-Zalessow's *Scrittici italiane dal XIII al XX secolo* (Ravenna: Longo editore, 1982). Thanks to Jim Carolan for help in biography preparation and to students in Beverly Allen's class on Italian women poets at Stanford University in 1983 for their interest and comments.

CONTENTS

*It seems to me that in a completely poetic land whose language
is both the noblest and the sweetest, all possible different paths
may be tried, and that, since the land of Alfieri and Monti has
not lost its ancient valor, on all of these paths she should be the
first.*

Diodata Saluzzo Roero

Blood is red so that you may see it.

Marta Fabiani

Those of us who have put together the volumes in this series have been
faced with similar problems concerning traditional national literary canons
and feminism. To my mind, there are two central questions. First, what
can be considered feminist in a diverse body of literature collected from
seven centuries of writing? Second, is there something that distinguishes
the feminism of contemporary poetry as a whole from the works of earlier
poets? The answers to these two questions, I believe, have to do with the
complex fact of writing. For example, whatever the historical context, the
fact that these poems were written at all may itself be viewed as a feminist
act. Further, the recognition in our time of this writing as an empowering
feminist act may be the key difference between our contemporaries and
those who came before. Let me elaborate.

In Italy, as elsewhere, traditional literary canons are male dominated,
as is control of publication. Yet there are certain characteristics of the Italian
situation which are unique. One is the fact that feminist poetry is not the
only literary production to have been marginalized by the traditional
canon. A rich body of dialect literature has also existed since the beginning
of the Italian language, giving a perspective from which the aulic works
are revealed as an option, an opting *for* the aulic. The inclusion of one or
two dialect poets in most anthologies of Italian literature may be seen as
a co-opting of the critical power of dialect literature, a strategy aimed at
avoiding the question of whether the traditional canon should stand as
it is. Something like this has happened with women's writing in Italy, too.
Although it has existed for as long as female literacy has been allowed,
its challenges to traditional principles have been effectively avoided. The
token inclusion in the canon of certain texts, such as the sonnets of **La
Compiuta Donzella*** (thirteenth century) or those of the female poets of
the cinquecento, fails to give the other context for those works, the
continuum of women's writing.

*The names of poets whose works are included in this volume appear in boldface type
at first mention.

Another important aspect of the Italian situation is the long-standing bond between women writers and the poetic genre, a bond again in vivid evidence in the Italian feminist movement since the 1960s. Women writing in Italian have excelled in all genres, and three in particular stand out: the epistle, the modern novel, and poetry. As we can see from the letters of **Vittoria Colonna** (1490–1547) to Michelangelo in the sixteenth century and **Sibilla Aleramo** (1876–1960) to Vincenzo Cardarelli and Dino Campana in our time, to mention but two examples, women have been brilliantly adept in the intimacy and immediacy of the epistolary genre. For all the lettered art and soul of Italian women we could take as emblem the passionate works of the fourteenth-century writer, Saint Catherine of Siena. Her letters reveal a political clout strong enough to influence the papacy's return from Avignon to Rome and also an affective intelligence, or erotic motivation, which has given us a timeless expression of female desire. The modern novel, as well, owes much to one of its earliest female practitioners, Grazia Deledda, who brought Italy its first Nobel Prize for literature in 1926, and is unthinkable without the contributions of such others as Matilde Serao, Natalia Ginzburg, and Elsa Morante, known for her rich representations of a consciousness other than the privileged one and her effective revisionary readings of modern history.

It is poetry, however, that provides us with the most complete history of women's writing in Italy. For centuries, Italian women have chosen poetry as their preferred mode of literary expression. The historical bond of woman to poem may be due to the fact that the poem depends on itself in much the same way as does a person who writes, perhaps especially a woman who writes. Striving within a largely male-determined realm, women have often been best aided by just the means the poem has to offer: a honing of subjective awareness and a complementary recognition of subjective predicaments in objective situations. The poem, like the feminist, perhaps, makes subjectivity problematic as it represents or as it works to avoid representing it.

Of course the facts of Italy's social history and the effects that history has had on the availability of women's texts preordain much of what is available to us. The relative paucity of selections here from the thirteenth, fourteenth, seventeenth, and eighteenth centuries reflects the fact that relatively few such texts are available to us, either because few women wrote during those periods or because much of what women did write was not preserved. The reasons for this extend beyond generic preference to considerations of sociohistorical context. We need only recall the low rate of literacy even among men of the ruling class in the late Middle Ages to marvel at the existence of a thirteenth-century woman such as La Compiuta Donzella who was not only literate but also a most able practitioner of the sonnet form. The odds against such a phenomenon are so great as to suggest to some that she was not a woman at all but a man using a pseudonym. We may reject this notion not only on the factual basis of a letter written to her by her contemporary, Guittone D'Arezzo, but also in the conviction that much of women's writing through the centuries lies buried in male-determined notions of propriety. As Virginia Woolf suggests, we may often assume that Anonymous herself was a woman.

Literacy was no guarantee against oppression and violence. In the sixteenth century, some aristocratic women, benefitting from the ideology of the preceding century's humanist movement, received training at an academy such as that of Vittorini da Feltre in Mantua, which was open to both sexes. More usually, daughters of wealthy or noble families were tutored at home. The classics, music, and poetry these women studied may have helped to prepare them for the early widowhood which was still often their lot. But it certainly did little to lessen the potential for violence of their highly civilized society or the difficult place of women within it, as we can see in the grieving poems of Vittoria Colonna; in "Liberty" by **Chiara Matraini** (1514–c.1597) (where Matraini may be referring less to her personal situation than to the Spanish threat to her native Lucca or the despotism of church and state that followed the Inquisition in 1540); in the distressed statement of **Laura Terracina** (1519–1577) that "if I unlearned, young and woman am, / I can have no good beginning nor good end"; and in the parodistic play on writing and duelling by **Veronica Franco** (1546–1591). **Modesta dal Pozzo** (1555–1592) points out the inequalities inherent in sixteenth century educational practice when she says:

> If when a daughter's to a father born,
> He would set her with his son to equal tasks,
> She would not in lofty enterprise or light
> Inferior be to brother or unequal.

Women did participate, nevertheless, in the erudite projects of fifteenth-century humanism and in the intellectual and courtly life of the Renaissance. The quattrocento gives us Tarquinia Molza's translations of Plato, for example, as well as Isotta Nogarola's dialogue on whether Adam or Eve had committed the greater sin. Nogarola, who wrote in both Latin and Italian, and her sister, Ginevra, Veronese noblewomen, were considered exemplary Renaissance women. The "question of women" (their nature and their role in society) debated in courtly circles reaches an apex in Baldassare Castiglione's *The Courtier*, where one of the interlocutors is Castiglione's promoter at the court of Urbino, Elisabetta Gonzaga (d. 1432), whose intellectual participation was highly respected. And in Ferrara, to mention another instance of the presence of powerful noblewomen, Eleanora D'Aragona (d. 1493), wife of Ercole I d'Este, and her daughter, Isabella d'Este (d. 1539), appear as active promoters of literary and artistic activity. The debates about women's roles continue during the seventeenth century; in 1622, for example, the intellectual Elena

Tarabotti (Suor Archangela) wrote on the problem of forcing women to become nuns. These are but a few instances of women's participation in the scholarship, patronage, and debates that, along with the systemic inequities described above, characterize the Renaissance in Italy.

The first Papal index of prohibited books appeared in 1557, and repressive policies governing publication during the Counter Reformation did nothing to hasten the enfranchisement, so to speak, of women writers. The only Italian city to maintain its independence from Papal authority throughout the sixteenth century was Venice. It should not be surprising, therefore, that Venice was the home of three of the most prolific of that century's female poets, **Gaspara Stampa** (c. 1523–1554), Veronica Franco, and Modesta dal Pozzo. However, to think of their situations and the role of the courtesan (which permitted Gaspara Stampa and Veronica Franco access to intellectual life) as easy would certainly be to exaggerate. Given similar repressive policies, including the continuation of the index, in the seventeenth century, many writers turned to the highly formalized artifice and conventions of the literary movement known as Arcadia, with its Petrarchan and Anacreontic posturings. In addition, literacy during the Baroque Era in Italy was still almost exclusively a privilege of the upper classes, as it has remained until our own century. To whatever extent the lyric had been established by the great women poets of the Italian Renaissance as a genre in which even female authors could receive some recognition, this status was greatly diminished during the seventeenth and eighteenth centuries. Not only did the social position of women remain oppressed, as we may read in the lament of **Petronilla Paolini Massimi** (1663–1726) about her marriage at the age of ten to a relative of Pope Clement X, but the possibilities of intellectual engagement and artistic production continued to be severely limited. In the Baroque and Enlightenment periods women were able to participate in literary life chiefly through their personal associations with men. The fact that **Faustina Maratti Zappi** (1680–1745) was accepted as a member of Arcadian literary society, for example, is due as much to the entry accorded her by her poet-husband's fame as it is to her own talent.

Things changed somewhat during the grand sweep of Romanticism, with its opening toward a wider European context in the late eighteenth and early nineteenth centuries. The Romantic women poets deftly adopted notions of the cult of the individual, the signifying power of nature, and intuitions of the sublime in their lyric representations, as we can see in "Suffering" by **Maria Guacci Nobile** (1808–1848) and in the extract included here from "The Heavens" by **Caterina Bon Brenzoni** (1813–1856). The way for this more active participation had been prepared to a certain extent by the international nature of Romantic aesthetic polemics. **Deodata Saluzzo Roero** (1774–1840), who was published in Turin, attracted the admiration not only of Italians such as Vittorio Alfieri,

Ugo Foscolo, and Alessandro Manzoni, but also of Alphonse de Lamartine and Madame de Staël. The Italian Romantic theorist, Ludovico di Breme, wrote that her opus contained an example of the "perfect romantic lyric."

In the nineteenth century more women writers participated in literary movements. In addition to her lyrics, for example, **Erminia Fuà Fusinato** (1834–1876) wrote patriotic verse in the nationalistic spirit of the Risorgimento. And the *decadentismo* (decadentism) of the late nineteenth and early twentieth centuries shows up vividly in the poetry of **La Contessa Lara** (1849–1896), **Vittoria Aganoor Pompili** (1855–1910), **Annie Vivanti** (1868–1942), **Ada Negri** (1870–1945), and Sibilla Aleramo. The beginnings of a recognizably modern feminist discourse, and the first texts to appear from any but upper-class women, are those of Annie Vivanti, Ada Negri, Sibilla Aleramo, and **Amelia Guglielminetti** (1885–1941). Sibilla Aleramo's life and work, in particular, today seem quintessentially feminist. Having left her husband and son in the Papal States of the Marche, Aleramo went north to Rome, where she eked out a living as a journalist, critic, novelist, and poet, insisting in her life and work on the positive cognitive value of feminine and feminist emotion. Like her friend Garbriele D'Annunzio, she was tinged by an involvement with fascism, one occasioned, in her case, by her desire to obtain a state pension in order to mitigate the near-poverty which was almost constantly her lot. In an ideological switch not uncommon at the time, Aleramo joined the Communist party just after the Second World War. Until her death in 1960, Aleramo worked as a militant political activist to alleviate the wretched conditions of the urban poor and to reform the social institutions and attitudes, including traditional notions of proper sexual comportment, that have historically oppressed Italian women.

In spite of the aesthetic distance between present-day post-modernism and turn-of-the-century decadentism, the writers of the late nineteenth and early twentieth centuries evince something resembling our late-twentieth-century feminism: that is, a consciousness not only of injustice and oppression but also of history and historical analysis, revolt, tactics, and relational ethics.

The popular songs from the late nineteenth and early twentieth centuries, however, illustrate a current of lament which can be found in the utterances of women throughout Italian oral tradition. This popular tradition, unlike the literary one, is not bound to conditions of literacy or the status of upper-class women and hence contains themes not often found in pre-twentieth-century written poetry. Complaints about dismal working conditions and economic situations, for example, appear along with complaints about family roles. Another important aspect of these songs should not be overlooked: their emphasis on the figure of the mother and, by extension, the world of women. In spite of everything, Italian women have often had at least a certain amount of domestic power and, to a large extent, have shaped the traditional extended family in Italy until recently. This world of women was a storehouse of inherited wisdom and close support, and its weakening due to wars, emigration, and Italy's changing economic topography has been partly restored outside traditional family structures by cooperative feminist efforts, especially in urban centers in central and northern Italy.

The twentieth-century poets represented in this anthology introduce a remarkable expansion of themes. This thematic wealth is an indication of the ways in which Italian feminist poets participate in international intellectual currents. For example, psychoanalytic theory and the resultant attention given to language inform the work of many of these writers. A few instances of this are the multilingual subjectivity of **Amelia Rosselli** (1930–) in "On Fatherish Men," originally written in English; the anti-Oedipal configurations of **Mariella Bettarini** (1942–) in "Paternal"; and "We Must Free Ourselves Today" by **Ida Vallerugo** (1943–). A feminist claim to eros is made by **Giulia Niccolai** (1934–) in "GN Is Happy" and by **Marianna Fiore** (1948–) in "You Opened a Door," to mention but two instances. Lovemaking, women loving men, and women loving women are also themes in the work of **Armanda Guiducci** (1923–), **Maria Luisa Spaziani** (1924–), **Biancamaria Frabotta** (1946–), **Vivian Lamarque** (1946–), and **Gabriella Sica** (1950–), while biological relationships and choices related to maternity are especially present in poems by **Margherita Guidacci** (1921–), **Anna Malfaiera** (1926–), **Rosanna Guerrini** (1935–), and Mariella Bettarini.

Thematic categories give but a partial picture, however; they fall short of indicating not only the intertwining of many themes in any one poet's lyric vision but also the inextricable links between theme and style so important to contemporary feminist consciousness. As stated earlier, these contemporary poets are conscious of their own feminism and thus work within a context not previously available to the same extent to female poets. This is most overtly apparent in such poems as "The Spiral Staircase" by **Liana Catri** (1929–) or "This Rage" by **Silvia Batisti** (1949–). But this consciousness is also characterized by the value it gives to what we might call the adventures of everyday life, the notion, that is, of everyday life as the real challenge facing us, which we find in the poems of **Patrizia Cavalli** (1947–), Maria Luisa Spaziani, and **Jolanda Insana** (1937–). In many of these poets' works, this notion arrives in the stylistic guise of free verse, the verse which could so easily slip into prose, the verse which Spaziani believes is most difficult for and most essential to the lyric of our time. No part of this contemporary poetry is unfamiliar with either feminist consciousness or the implications of formal poetic practices. In "Poems by Women," for example, **Dacia Maraini** (1936–) argues against formal sophistication:

> A woman who writes poetry and knows that
> she is a woman can only make herself stick

closely to the subject because sophistication
of form is something that goes with power
and the power a woman has is always a
non-power, a burning inheritance never wholly hers.

Marta Fabiani (1953–) discusses thematic discretion with violence and irony in "The Poetess":

The poetess weaves tapestries
in a seditious lodging [. . .]
We must be nice, she says.
We must be discreet: so that she never hurls in your face
her foot fetish
never offers you
her great sore to lick.
Blood is red so that you may see it [. . .]
It is still her job
to count the chambers in the pistol
to be sure everything is in order,
accountant even in this hateful occupation.

Finally, in "The Death of Poetry," **Livia Candiani** (1952–) marks an end of poetry "without history," an end which is also her own, but from which she revives, having traveled through her body into an external world of great suffering and liberating change. She writes:

my death
stopped traveling
and I have emerged
from a larger and heavier
new placenta
the historic placenta
and have begun to scream
with the redness of my rage

Contemporary feminist poetry in Italy is marked by this sense of history which is also a recognition of the power of the poetic word in a culture where words make history. If the poems of earlier female poets have been denied their place in literary tradition, the poems of the contemporary poets now give voice not only to a new consciousness but also to a new history, a history that claims the power of poetry as its own.

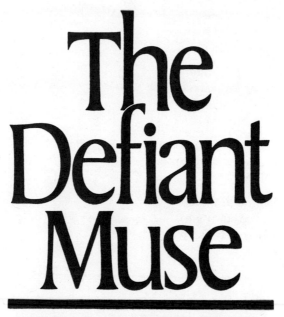

The Defiant Muse

ITALIAN FEMINIST POEMS
FROM THE MIDDLE AGES
TO THE PRESENT

TAPINA AHIMÈ, CH'AMAVA UNO SPARVIERO

Tapina ahimè, ch'amava uno sparviero:
amaval tanto ch'io me ne moria;
a lo richiamo ben m'era manero,
e dunque troppo pascer nol dovia.

Or è montato e salito sì altero,
as[s]ai più alto che far non solia,
ed è asiso dentro a uno verzero:
un'altra donna lo tene in balìa.

Isparvero mio, ch'io t'avea nodrito,
sonaglio d'oro ti facea portare
perché dell'ucellar fosse più ardito:

or se' salito sì come lo mare,
ed ha' rotti li geti e se' fugito,
quando eri fermo nel tuo ucellare.

A LA STAGION CHE 'L MONDO FOGLIA E FIORA

A la stagion che 'l mondo foglia e fiora
acresce gioia a tuti fin' amanti:
vanno insieme a li giardini alora
che gli auscelletti fanno dolzi canti;

la franca gente tutta s'inamora,
e di servir ciascun trages' inanti,
ed ogni damigella in gioia dimora;
e me, n'abondan marimenti e pianti.

Ca lo mio padre m'ha messa 'n errore,
e tenemi sovente in forte doglia:
donar mi vole a mia forza segnore,

ed io di ciò non ho disio né voglia,
e 'n gran tormento vivo a tutte l'ore;
però non mi ralegra fior né foglia.

ANONYMOUS (THIRTEENTH CENTURY)

AH WRETCHED ME, WHO LOVED A SPARROW HAWK

Ah wretched me, who loved a sparrow hawk;
so loved him I was dying for his love;
well was he gentled to my command
and I never had to feed him overmuch.

Now most proudly has he flown and risen
much higher than he was wont to do,
and within an orchard has he made his perch,
another woman does control him now.

My sparrow-hawk, I nurtured you,
a golden bell I gave you to wear
that you might be bolder in your falconry:

now you have risen like the sea
and burst your chains and fled away,
though you were safe and sound inside your aviary.

LA COMPIUTA DONZELLA (THIRTEENTH CENTURY)

IN THE SEASON WHEN THE WORLD'S IN LEAF AND FLOWER

In the season when the world's in leaf and flower
the joy of all true lovers waxes strong:
in pairs they go to gardens at the hour
when little birds are singing their sweet song;

All gentle folk now come beneath love's power,
and the service of his love is each man's care,
while every maid in gladness spends her hours;
but I am filled with weeping and despair.

For my father has treated me most ill
and keeps me often in the sorest anguish:
he would give me to a lord against my will.

And this I neither do desire nor wish,
and every hour I pass in sharpest grief;
and so receive no joy from flower or leaf.

LASCIAR VORIA LO MONDO E DIO SERVIRE

Lasciar voria lo mondo e Dio servire
e dipartirmi d'ogne vanitate,
però che vegio crescere e salire
matezza e villania e falsitate,

ed ancor senno e cortesia morire
e lo fin pregio e tutta la bontate:
ond'io marito non voria né sire,
né stare al mondo, per mia volontate.

Membrandomi c'ogn'om di mal s'adorna,
di ciaschedun son forte disdegnosa,
e verso Dio la mia persona torna.

Lo padre mio mi fa stare pensosa,
ca di servire a Cristo mi distorna:
non saccio a cui mi vol dar per isposa.

POI CHE PER MIA VENTURA A VEDER TORNO

Poi che per mia ventura a veder torno
voi, dolci colli, e voi, chiare e fresch'acque,
e tu, che tanto a la natura piacque
farti, sito gentil, vago e adorno,

ben posso dire avventuroso il giorno,
e lodar sempre quel desio che nacque
in me di rivedervi, che pria giacque
morto nel cor di dolor cinto intorno.

Vi veggi' or dunque, e tal dolcezza sento,
che quante mai da la fortuna offese
ricevute ho finor, pongo in oblio.

Così sempre vi sia largo e cortese,
lochi beati, il ciel, come in me spento
è, se non di voi soli, ogni desio.

THIS WORLD I'D WISH TO LEAVE AND GOD TO SERVE

This world I'd wish to leave and God to serve
and myself to sever from all vanity,
because the growth and increase I observe
of falsehood, foolishness, and villainy.

Good sense and courtesy also expire,
high excellence and generosity;
wherefore no lord nor husband I desire
nor in the world remain now willingly.

Seeing that evil by every man is worn,
all of them I do disdain,
and toward God my self I turn.

My father fills me with an anxious pain
for from serving Christ he does prevent me:
I know not to what lord he wants to give me.

VERONICA GAMBARA   (1485–1550)

SINCE I, BY MY GOOD FORTUNE, RETURN TO LOOK ON

Since I, by my good fortune, return to look on
you, sweet hills, and you, waters cool and clear,
and you, gracious site, whom it much pleased
nature to make adorned and fair,

I can indeed call fortunate the day
and ever praise the longing that was born
in me to look on you again, that earlier lay
dead in my heart ringed around with pain.

You then, I look on now, and such sweetness feel
that however many blows from fortune
I've hitherto received, I forget them now.

And so, ever generous and kind
to you, blest places, may heaven be, while in me
desire is spent except for you alone.

SCRIVO SOL PER SFOGAR L'INTERNA DOGLIA

Scrivo sol per sfogar l'interna doglia,
di che si pasce il cor, ch'altro non vole,
e non per giunger lume al mio bel sole,
che lasciò in terra sí onorata spoglia.

Giusta cagione a lamentar m'invoglia;
ch'io scemi la sua gloria assai mi dole;
per altra penna e piú saggie parole
verrà chi a morte il suo gran nome toglia.

La pura fé, l'ardor, l'intensa pena
mi scusi appo ciascun, grave cotanto
che né ragion né tempo mai l'affrena.

Amaro lagrimar, non dolce canto,
foschi sospiri e non voce serena,
di stil no, ma di duol mi danno il vanto.

PROVO TRA DURI SCOGLI E FIERO VENTO

Provo tra duri scogli e fiero vento
l'onde di questa vita in fragil legno;
e non ho piú a guidarlo arte né ingegno:
quasi è al mio scampo ogni soccorso lento.

Spense l'acerba morte in un momento
quel ch'era la mia stella e 'l chiaro segno:
or contro 'l mar turbato e l'aer pregno
non ho piú aita; anzi piú ognor pavento.

Non di dolce cantar d'empie sirene;
non di romper tra queste altere sponde;
non di fondar nelle commosse arene;

ma sol di navigare ancor queste onde,
che tanto tempo solco e senza spene:
ché il fido porto mio morte m'asconde.

VITTORIA COLONNA   (1490–1547)

I WRITE ONLY TO RELIEVE MY INNER GRIEF

I write only to relieve my inner grief,
on which my heart, that wants no other food, does feed,
and not to contribute light to my great sun
who left on earth much-honored last remains.

A just cause does lead me to lament;
but it grieves me that I may lessen his bright fame;
someone with other pen and better words
shall come to steal from death my lord's proud name.

Let true faith and ardor make my excuse to all
for my intense distress, so heavy
that neither time nor reason can e'er make less

Bitter weeping, not sweet poetry,
dismal sighs and not a voice serene,
for grief, and not for style, do bring me praise.

BETWEEN HARD ROCKS AND SAVAGE WINDS I TRY

Between hard rocks and savage winds I try
the waters of this life in fragile craft;
no longer have I art nor skill to steer:
it seems no help for my relief comes nigh.

Spent in a moment by harsh death is he
who was my star and my direction clear:
now 'gainst teeming air and wrathful sea
I've no more aid, but everywhere more fear;

Not fear of wicked sirens' sweetest song;
not fear of shipwreck between these lofty shores;
not fear of foundering in the swirling sands;

fear only still to navigate these waves
that I have plowed so hopelessly and long,
because death hides from me my haven sure.

LA LIBERTÀ

Mai, fuor di libertà, dolce nè cara
cosa non fu, nè fia bella e gradita,
onde il buon Cato prima uscir di vita
volle che servitute empia ed amara.

Felice quel che a l'altrui esempio impara,
e la grazia di Dio larga infinita
conosce e gode, anzi che sia partita
la sua tranquillità serena e chiara.

Io, da che sciolta e rotta la catena
sento, onde fui sì strettamente avvolta,
non fia giammai ch'io sia più per entrarve,

ch'ombre diverse e spaventose larve
mi son d'intorno al cor con sì gran pena
qualor vi penso, ch'a fuggir son volta.

da *IL DISCORSO SOPRA IL PRINCIPIO DI TUTTI I CANTI DI
ORLANDO FURIOSO*

ALLA ECCELLENT. SIGNORA VERONICA GAMBARA

Deh fosser molte al mondo come voi,
donne che a gli scrittor mettesser freno,
ch'a tutta briglia vergan contra noi
scritti crudeli e colmi di veleno:
ché forse andrebbe insino ai liti Eoi
il nome nostro e 'l grido d'onor pieno.
Ma perché contra a lor nulla si mostra,
però tengono vil la fama nostra.

CHIARA MATRAINI (1514–c. 1597)

LIBERTY

   Naught but liberty was ever
sweet and dear, nor shall pleasing be or fair;
wherefore good Cato chose his life to sever
and no evil bitter servitude to bear.

   Happy the man who from example learns,
and knows and enjoys the grace of God,
so wide and infinite, before his own
serene and clear tranquility departs.

   Since broken now and loosed I feel the chain
that round about me was so tightly wound,
may I never chance to enter it again,

   for diverse shadows and terrifying ghosts
surround my heart with such great pain,
whene'er I think of it, that to flee I'm bound.

LAURA TERRACINA (c. 1519–c.1577)

from *THE DISCOURSE ON THE PRINCIPLE IN ALL THE CANTOS OF ORLANDO FURIOSO*

TO THE MOST EXCELLENT LADY VERONICA GAMBARA

Ah! would there were many in the world like you,
women who would set a curb on men
who rush headlong to compose against us
cruel writings, filled with venom—
lest as far, perhaps, as Oriental shores might go
our name and fame with honor laden.
But because no woman comes to challenge them
they hold our reputation in contempt.

COMMIATO

Qualunque sia che per caso o per forza
legga giammai queste mie incolte rime
benchè l'onore e il giudicio lo sforza
sì, che convien ch'assai poco le stime;
pur lo pregh'io che non passi la scorza,
chè l'ignoranza mia dentro s'imprime:
e, se giovane, indotta, e donna io sono,
nè principio nè fin posso aver buono.

POSCIA CH'AL BEL DESIR TRONCANTE HAI L'ALE

Poscia ch'al bel desir troncate hai l'ale,
che nel mio cor sorgea, crudel Fortuna,
sí che d'ogni tuo ben vivo digiuna,
dirò con questo stil ruvido e frale
alcuna parte de l'interno male
causato sol da te fra questi dumi,
fra questi aspri costumi
di gente irrazional, priva d'ingegno,
ove senza sostegno
son costretta a menare il viver mio,
qui posta da ciascuno in cieco oblio.

Tu, crudel, de l'infanzia in quei pochi anni,
del caro genitor mi festi priva,
che, se non è già pur ne l'altra riva,
per me sente di morte i gravi affanni,
ché 'l mio penar raddoppia gli suoi danni.
Cesar gli vieta il poter darmi aita.

O cosa non piú udita,
privare il padre di giovar la figlia!
Cosí, a disciolta briglia,
seguitata m'hai sempre, empia Fortuna,
cominciando dal latte e da la cuna.

ENVOI TO POEM TO THE VIRGIN

Whoever may by chance or of necessity
read some day these uncouth lines of mine,
though he may be compelled by honor and good sense
to consider them in rather low esteem,
I beg that he probe not beneath the skin,
because my ignorance makes its mark within:
and if I am young, unlearnèd, and a woman,
I can have no good beginning nor good end.

ISABELLA DI MORRA   (1520–1546)

SINCE YOU HAVE CLIPPED THE WINGS OF FINE DESIRE

Since you have clipped the wings of fine desire
lest it spring within my heart, oh cruel Fortune,
so that I live deprived of all your gifts,
I'll tell in this crude and feeble style
some part of the internal ill
caused only by you among these briars,
among these harsh customs
of an irrational race bereft of wit,
where I without support
am here constrained to pass my life,
left by everyone in dark oblivion.

Cruel one, in those few years of infancy
you caused my dear sire to be taken from me,
who, though not indeed crossed to the other shore,
yet feels for me the heavy pangs of death,
since my suffering doubles his own griefs.
Caesar denies him power to give me aid.

Oh thing unheard of:
to prevent a father from succoring his child!
Thus in headlong haste,
oh pitiless Fortune, have you pursued me ever,
beginning with the breast and in the cradle.

Quella ch'è detta la fiorita etade,
secca ed oscura, solitaria ed erma
tutta ho passato qui cieca ed inferma,
senza saper mai pregio di beltade.
È stata per me morta in te pietade,
e spenta l'hai in altrui, che potea sciorre
e in altra parte porre
del carcer duro il vel de l'alma stanca,
che, come neve bianca
dal sol, cosí da te si strugge ogn'ora,
e struggerassi infin che qui dimora.

Qui non provo io di donna il proprio stato
per te, che posta m'hai in sí ria sorte
che dolce vita mi saria la morte.
I cari pegni del mio padre amato
piangon d'intorno. Ahi, ahi! misero fato,
mangiare il frutto c'altri colse, amaro
quei che mai non peccaro,
la cui semplicità faria clemente
una tigre, un serpente,
ma non già te, vêr noi piú fiera e rea
c'al figlio Progne ed al fratel Medea.

Dei ben, ch'ingiustamente la tua mano
dispensa, fatta m'hai tanto mendica
che mostri ben quanto mi sei nemica,
in questo inferno solitario e strano
ogni disegno mio facendo vano.
S'io mi doglio di te sí giustamente
per isfogar la mente,
da chi non son per ignoranza intesa
i' son, lassa, ripresa:
ché, se nodrita già fossi in cittade,
avresti tu piú biasmo, io piú pietade.

Bastone i figli de la fral vecchiezza
esser dovean di mia misera madre;
ma per le tue procelle inique ed acre
sono in estrema ed orrida fiacchezza;
e spenta in lor sarà la gentilezza
dagli antichi lasciata, a questi giorni,
se dagli alti soggiorni

That time that's called the age of flowering,
I, dry and dark, solitary and alone,
have spent entirely here, blind and ill,
and never knew what beauty meant.
In you pity for me has died
and you have quenched it in him who could save,
and carry to another place away
from this harsh prison, the veil of my tired soul,
which, as white snow
by the sun, so by you each hour is destroyed
and will be destroyed as long as it stays here.

Here, woman's rightful place I do not enjoy,
through you, who have cast me so dire a lot
that death for me would be a pleasing life.
The dear pledges of my beloved sire
weep around me. Alas, what wretched fate
to eat the fruit another plucked, bitter
to those who never sinned,
whose simplicity would render merciful
a tigress or a snake,
but never you, to us more fierce and cruel
than Procne to her son, or Medea to her brother.*

Of good things, which unjustly your hand
dispenses, you have so beggared me
that you clearly prove how much you are my enemy,
in this strange and solitary hell,
making futile all my plans.
If I complain of you so justly
to relieve my mind,
alas, I am censured
by those who through ignorance misunderstand me:
for, had I indeed been bred within a city,
you would have had more blame and I more pity.

Of frail old age her sons should be
the supports of my unhappy mother;
but through your black and wicked storms
they are in dire and utter weakness;
and quenched in them will be gentility
bequeathed from ancient days to these,
unless from the high heavens

*According to Greek mythology, Procne killed her son Itys and served him to his
father, Tereus, for dinner, to avenge the rape of her sister by Tereus; Medea killed her
brother and fled with Jason, her husband.

pietà non giugne al cor del re di Francia,
che, con giusta bilancia
pesando il danno, agguaglie la mercede
secondo il merto di mia pura fede.

Ogni mal ti perdono,
né l'alma si dorrà di te giammai
se questo sol farai
—ahi, ahi, Fortuna, e perché far nol dei?—
che giungano al gran Re gli sospir miei.

IO SON DA L'ASPETTAR ORMAI SÍ STANCA

Io son da l'aspettar ormai sí stanca,
sí vinta dal dolor e dal disio,
per la sí poca fede e molto oblio
di chi del suo tornar, lassa, mi manca,

che lei, che 'l mondo impalidisce e 'mbianca
con la sua falce e dà l'ultimo fio,
chiamo talor per refrigerio mio,
sí 'l dolor nel mio petto si rinfranca.

Ed ella si fa sorda al mio chiamare,
schernendo i miei pensier fallaci e folli,
come sta sordo anch'egli al suo tornare.

Cosí col pianto, ond'ho gli occhi miei molli,
fo pietose quest'onde e questo mare;
ed ei si vive lieto ne' suoi colli.

pity reach the heart of France's king,
so that, with equal scales
weighing the injury, he make just reward
according to the merit of my blameless faith.

Every evil I forgive you,
nor shall my soul ever complain of you
if you will do this only—
Ah, Ah, Fortune, and why should you not?—
let my sighs come unto the great King?

GASPARA STAMPA   (c. 1523–1554)

BY NOW I AM SO TIRED OF WAITING

By now I am so tired of waiting,
so overcome by longing and by grief,
through the so little faith and much forgetting
of him of whose return I, weary, am bereaved,

that she who makes the world pale, whitening
it with her sickle, and claims the final forfeit—
I call on her often for relief,
so strongly sorrow wells within my breast.

But she turns deaf ears unto my plea,
scorning my false and foolish thoughts,
as he to his return stays also deaf.

And so with weeping whence my eyes are filled,
I make piteous these waters and this sea;
while he lives happy there upon his hills.

CONTE, DOV'È ANDATA

Conte, dov'è andata
la fé sí tosto, che m'avete data?
Che vuol dir che la mia
è piú costante, che non era pria?
Che vuol dir che, da poi
che voi partiste, io son sempre con voi?
Sapete voi quel che dirà la gente,
dove forza d'Amor punto si sente?
—O che conte crudele!
o che donna fedele!—

SPOGLIATA E SOLA E INCAUTA MI COGLIESTE

Spogliata e sola e incauta mi coglieste,
debil d'animo, e in armi non esperta,
e robusto ed armato m'offendeste;

tanto ch'io stèi per lungo spazio incerta
di mia salute; e fu da me tra tanto
passion infinita al cor sofferta.

Pur finalmente s'è stagnato il pianto,
e quella piaga acerba s'è saldata,
che da l'un mi passava a l'altro canto.

Quasi da pigro sonno or poi svegliata,
dal cansato periglio animo presi,
benché femina a molli opere nata;

e in man col ferro a esercitarmi appresi,
tanto ch'aver le donne agil natura,
non men che l'uomo, in armeggiando intesi:

perchè 'n ciò posto ogni mia industria e cura,
mercè del ciel, mi veggo giunta a tale,
che più d'offese altrui non ho paura.

OH COUNT, WHERE HAS GONE

Oh Count, where has gone
So soon the faith you swore?
What does it mean that mine
Is more constant than before?
What does it mean that since
You left I'm always with you?
Do you know what folk will say
Who feel Love's power at all?
"Oh, how the Count is cruel!
Oh, how the lady is true!"

VERONICA FRANCO (1546–1591)

NAKED AND ALONE AND UNWARY YOU CAUGHT ME

Naked and alone and unwary you caught me,
feeble of spirit and in arms untried,
while strong and armed yourself you did attack me;

so that of my health I did abide
long uncertain: and suffered in my heart
an infinite passion all the while.

But stemmed finally were my tears,
and that bitter wound was healed
which me from side to side had pierced.

Now nearly roused from slothful sleep,
from past danger I have extracted boldness,
although a woman born to gentle deeds;

and with sword in hand often exercised,
until I found that in feats of arms
woman's agility is no less than man's:

in this I set all industry and care,
and so, thanks to heaven, am come to such a pass
that attacks from others I no longer fear.

E, se voi dianzi mi trattaste male,
fu gran vostro difetto, ed io dal danno
grave n'ho tratto un ben, che molto vale. [. . .]

Di ciò non se ne son le donne accorte;
chè, se si risolvessero di farlo,
con voi pugnar porrìan fino a la morte.

E per farvi veder che 'l vero parlo,
tra tante donne incominciar voglio io,
porgendo esempio a lor di seguitarlo.

A voi, che contra tutte sète rio,
con qual'armi volete in man mi volgo,
con speme d'atterrarvi e con desìo;

e le donne a difender tutte tolgo
contra di voi, che di lor sète schivo,
sì ch'a ragion io sola non mi dolgo.

Certo d'un gran piacer voi sète privo,
a non gustar di noi la gran dolcezza;
ed al mal uso in ciò la colpa ascrivo.

Data è dal ciel la feminil bellezza,
perch'ella sia felicitade in terra
di qualunque uom conosce gentilezza.

Ma dove 'l mio pensier trascorre ed erra
a ragionar de le cose d'amore,
or ch'io sono in procinto di far guerra?

Torno al mio intento, ond'era uscita fuore,
e vi disfido a singolar battaglia:
cingetevi pur d'armi e di valore,

vi mostrerò quanto al vostro prevaglia
il sesso femminil: pigliate quali
volete armi, e di voi stesso vi caglia,

ch'io vi risponderò di colpi tali,
il campo a voi lasciando elegger anco,
ch'a questi forse non sentiste eguali.

Mal difender da me potrete il fianco,
e stran vi parrà forse, a offenderne uso,
da me vedervi oppresso in terra stanco:

così talor quell'uom resta deluso,
ch'ingiuria gli altri fuor d'ogni ragione,
non so se per natura, o per mal uso.

And if you once injured me, then indeed gross
has been your fault, while I from that grave wrong
have gained a good that great value has. [...]

Though women may consider this a fable,
if they would but resolve to see it through,
then, to fight you to the death they would be able.

And to prove that I am speaking true
among so many women shall I go first,
giving example for them to follow too.

You, guilty towards them all, against
you I turn, taking whichever weapon you intend,
with hope and wish to bring you to the dust;

and I act to defend all women
from you who unto them are disinclined,
so much that I do not alone lament.

Truly much pleasure have you declined
by not enjoying our sweet quality;
and in ill use of this your guilt I find.

On earth to bring felicity
Heaven women's beauty does bestow,
for any man who knows true courtesy.

But whither strays my thought and wanders so
to talk of things of love's concern,
now when to war I am prepared to go?

To my initial purpose I return:
to single combat challenge you I dare:
though you gird yourself with arms and courage stern,

I shall show you how superior is by far
the female sex to yours: now choose
what arms you will, and yourself beware,

for I shall answer you with matching blows,
and as in these you may feel unequal
the field I also leave to you to choose.

To defend your flank from me you'll be ill able,
and, accustomed to attack, strange you may feel,
vanquished by me, on the ground and feeble:

thus sometimes is a man deluded still
who injures others beyond reason's aid,
whether from nature or bad habit I cannot tell.

Vostra di questa rissa è la cagione,
ed a me per difesa e per vendetta
carico d'oppugnarvi ora s'impone.

Prendete pur de l'armi omai l'eletta,
ch'io non posso soffrir lunga dimora,
da lo sdegno de l'animo costretta.

La spada, che 'n man vostra rade e fora,
de la lingua volgar veneziana,
s'a voi piace d'usar, piace a me ancòra:

e, se volete entrar ne la toscana,
scegliete voi la seria o la burlesca,
ché l'una e l'altra è a me facile e piana.

Io ho veduto in lingua selvagesca
certa fattura vostra molto bella,
simile a la maniera pedantesca: [...]

Per contrastar con voi con ardimento,
in tutte queste ho molta industria speso:
se bene o male, io stessa mi contento;

e ciò sarà dagli altri ancòra inteso,
e 'l saperete voi, che forse vinto
cadrete, e non vorreste avermi offeso. [...]

Apparecchiate pur l'inchiostro e 'l foglio,
e fatemi saper senz'altro indugio
quali armi per combatter in man toglio. [...]

The occasion for the quarrel you have made
and, for defense and in revenge, on me
the burden of attacking you is laid.

So take the now selected weaponry,
for I cannot suffer long delays,
my spirit's indignation urges me.

The sword that in your hand does pierce and graze,
that of the common Venetian tongue,
if you please to use, it me too shall please;

and if you wish to engage in Tuscan,
then either the serious or burlesque prefer,
since both for me are easy and are plain.

I have seen in tongue more popular
writings of yours that have much talent,
to the pedantic manner similar: [. . .]

In order to argue with you with bold intent,
in all of these I've spent much industry,
whether for good or ill, I am myself content;

And this by others understood shall be,
and this shall you know too, for perhaps you'll fall
defeated, wishing you had not attacked me. [. . .]

So ink and paper do you prepare withal,
and let me know without more delay
which weapons I should take up for the fray [. . .]

IL MERITO DELLE DONNE

Le donne in ogni età fur da Natura
  Di gran giudicio e d'animo dotate,
  Nè men atte a mostrar con studio e cura
  Senno e valor degli uomini son nate.
  E perchè, se comune è la figura,
  Se non son le sostanze variate,
  S'hanno simile un cibo e un parlar, denno
  Differente aver poi l'ardire e il senno?

Sempre s'è visto e vede, pur che alcuna
  Donna v'abbia voluto il pensier porre,
  Nella milizia riuscir più d'una
  E il pregio e il grido a molti uomini torre.
  E così nelle lettere e in ciascuna
  Impresa che l'uom pratica e discorre,
  Le donne sì buon frutto han fatto e fanno,
  Che gli uomini a invidiar punto non hanno.

E benchè di sè degno e sì famoso
  Grado, di lor non sia numero molto,
  È perchè ad atto eroico e virtuoso
  Non hanno il cor per più rispetti volto.
  L'oro che sta nelle minere ascoso
  Non lascia d'esser or benchè sepolto,
  E quando è tratto e se ne fa lavoro,
  È così ricco e bel come l'altro oro.

Se quando nasce una figliuola al padre,
  La ponesse col figlio a un'opra eguale,
  Non saria nelle imprese alte e leggiadre
  Al frate inferior nè disuguale;
  O la ponesse in fra le armate squadre
  Seco o a imparar qualch'arte liberale;
  Ma perchè in altri affar viene allevata,
  Per l'educazion poco è stimata.

MODESTA DAL POZZO (1555–1592)

WOMEN'S WORTH

Women in every age by Nature were
  With sound judgment and brave hearts endowed,
  And no less fit to demonstrate with zeal
  Men's wisdom, care, and worth, were born,
  And why then, if they bear a common stamp,
  If their substances be not different,
  If they have one food, one speech alike,
  Should they then differ in good sense and courage?

There have been always and still are (whene'er
  A woman decides to put her mind to it)
  Successful women warriors, more than one,
  Who wrest both prize and rank from many men;
  So too in letters and in every
  Enterprise man undertakes or speaks of,
  Women have been and are full well so fruitful
  That they have no cause to envy men.

And, though worthy in itself, their number
  In positions of high fame is not large;
  This is because to splendid and heroic acts
  They have not addressed their hearts in more respects.
  Gold left hidden deep within the mines
  Is no less gold for being buried there,
  And when extracted and well worked upon
  Is just as rich and fine as other gold.

If, when a daughter to a father is born,
  He were to set her with his son to equal tasks,
  She would not in lofty enterprise or light
  Inferior or unequal to her brother be;
  Or were he to place her in armed squadrons
  With him, or allow her to learn some liberal art;
  But because she is reared to other things,
  Small esteem her education brings.

da *SPIEGHI LE CHIOME IRATE*

FORTUNA ALFIN M'ACCOLSE

Fortuna alfin m'accolse,
e lungo stuol d'adorator divoti
i miei ricchi imenei chiedeva a gara;
ed oh quanti raccolse
lo splendor di mia sorte incensi e voti,
ch'adulando porgea la turba avara!
Già cominciava ad esser lieta e cara
a me la vita e l'aura era gentile,
e già l'alma e il pensier s'ergean sull'ale,
quando forza fatale
de gli anni miei congiunse il vago aprile
a strana età senile:
io rammentai colle mie nozze allora
l'ingrate tede all'infelice Aurora.

Del gran Pastor latino
l'alto voler fu legge a' miei sponsali,
e il cenno suo dettò il materno assenso.
Vide allora il destino,
al lume di mie faci nuziali,
estinta la pietà non ch'altro senso.
Del pianto mio, del mio dolore intenso
godero i fati e riser gli astri alteri,
che resero crudel Giove clemente;
ei di fasto apparente
coprì l'orrore; ed a i potenti imperi
cedero i miei pensieri
qual onda al vento; e tra l'illustri cure
sol potei numerar le mie sventure.   (ll. 85-112)

PETRONILLA PAOLINI MASSIMI (1663–1726)

from *UNBIND YOUR ANGERED TRESSES*

FORTUNE WELCOMED ME AT LAST

Fortune welcomed me at last,
and a long host of devoted admirers
strove to compete for my rich marriage;
and oh, how many vows and flatteries,
captured by the splendor of my station,
offered, fawning, that greedy crowd!
Already life was beginning to be joyful and precious
to me, and the air was gentle,
and already my mind and soul were rising on wings,
when the strong hand of fate
joined the fair April of my years
to an alien old age;
in my nuptials I then recalled
unfortunate Aurora's displeasing marriage.*

The great Latin Shepherd's**
lofty wish was my wedding's law,
and his nod dictated my mother's consent.
Destiny then witnessed
by the light of my nuptial torches
pity extinguished with all other feeling.
My tears, my deep distress
the Fates enjoyed, and those haughty stars laughed
who had made clement Jove cruel;
he with outward pomp
concealed the horror; and to his powerful commands
my thoughts surrendered
as a wave before the wind; and among illustrious duties
I could only enumerate my misfortunes.   (ll. 85-112)

*According to Greek mythology, Aurora, wife of Prince Tithon of Troy, persuaded Zeus
to grant Tithon immortality but forgot to ask for eternal youth. Her husband grew old,
and the goddess looked after him for a while but finally shut him up in a room, where
he was eventually changed into a cicada.
**Pope Clement X

SDEGNA CLORINDA A I FEMMINILI UFFICI

Sdegna Clorinda a i femminili uffici
chinar la destra, e sotto l'elmo accoglie
i biondi crini e con guerriere voglie
fa del proprio valor pompa a i nemici.

Così gli alti natali e i lieti auspici
e gli aurei tetti e le regali spoglie
nulla curando, Amalasonta coglie
de' fecondi Licei lauri felici.

Mente capace d'ogni nobil cura
ha il nostro sesso: or qual potente inganno
dall'imprese d'onor l'alme ne fura?

So ben che i fati a noi guerra non fanno,
né i suoi doni contende a noi natura:
sol del nostro valor l 'uomo è tiranno.

AL FIGLIUOLO RINALDO AMMALATO

Dov'è, dolce mio caro amato figlio,
il lieto sguardo e la fronte serena;
ove la bocca di bei vezzi piena,
e l'inarcar del grazïoso ciglio?

Ahimè, tu manchi sotto il fier periglio
di crudel morbo, che di vena in vena
ti scorre, e il puro sangue n'avvelena,
e già minaccia all'alma il lungo esiglio.

TO FEMALE DUTIES CLORINDA SCORNED

To female duties Clorinda* scorned
to turn her hand, and beneath her helmet gathered
her blond tresses and with warlike aims
herself displayed her worth to enemies.

   Likewise for lofty birth and joyful auspices,
for golden palaces and royal regalia
caring no whit, Amalasuntha** won
felicitous laurels from Athens' fruitful schools.

   A mind apt for every noble care
our sex possesses: so what mighty fraud
diverts our souls from deeds of honor?

   I well know the fates war not with us,
nor does Nature to us deny her gifts:
the sole oppressor of our worth is man.

*Clorinda is the Tasso heroine who was beloved and mistakenly put to death by
Tancredi. In the *Gerusalemme liberata* she is depicted as rejecting traditional female
activities in favor of exercise in arms.
**Amalasuntha was the daughter of Theodoric, king of the Ostrogoths. Upon her
father's death in 526, she obtained the throne for her son, Atalaric, who died in 534.
She was killed in 535 by her cousin, Theodatus, whom she had made king.
Amalasuntha received honors as a literary scholar.

FAUSTINA MARATTI ZAPPI (1680–1745)

TO HER LITTLE SON RINALDO WHEN SICK

   Oh where, my sweet, my dear beloved son,
is that happy look and that brow serene?
Where is that mouth so full of pleasing charms,
and the graceful eyebrow's curving arch?

   Alas, you sink beneath the peril grave
of cruel illness that, from vein to vein,
spreads through you and poisons your pure blood,
and now menaces your soul with long exile.

Ah, ch'io ben veggio, io veggio il tuo vicino
ultimo danno; e contro il Ciel mi lagno,
figlio, del mio, del tuo crudel destino:

e il duol tal del mio pianto al cor fa stagno,
che spesso al tuo bel volto io m'avvicino,
e né pur d'una lagrima lo bagno.

LA GUERRA DELL'ANNO MDCCXCIII

Bruna, bruna è la notte, or la nativa
Mia collinetta tutta copre; solo
Il piccioletto rio fugge piangendo
Entro verdifronzuta ascosa valle.
Canto simile al mormorio del rivo
Io scioglierò; da quelle fronde un lieve
Raggio di luna giù fra' bianchi veli
Del crin mi viene, sulla cetra scende:
È mesto il raggio, come or mesta sento
Tutta l'anima mia. La patria sorte
Copre nube funesta. Ahi! mute stanno
Abbandonate le paterne mura
Prive de' figli, e meco è sempre sempre
Malinconia, sacra pel cuore dei vati,
Che d'immagini nate entro 'l profondo
Seno è madre sublime. Ignota sono
Vergin sull'Alpi ancor; mi sorge appena
L'età del canto. Un dì sarò dell'Alpi
Il nobil vate, e nobil carme udranno
Sulla cetera i prodi: or canto solo
Onde destar pietà, vergine ignota
Abitatrice dei selvaggi monti.

Ah, how I clearly see, I see at hand your
final loss; and to Heaven I bewail,
oh son, my cruel destiny and yours:

and this grief so stems the weeping in my heart
that often I draw near your lovely face,
yet cannot bathe it in a single tear.

DIODATA SALUZZO (1774–1840)

THE WAR OF 1793*

Dark, dark is the night, now it wholly
Covers my native hillock; alone
The tiny stream flees away weeping
Within the green-leaved secret valley.
A song like the murmuring of the brook
Shall I sing; from these boughs a thin
Moonbeam through pallid wisps
Of hair reaches me, falls on my lyre:
Sad is the beam, sad as I now feel
My whole soul to be. A baleful cloud
Covers my country's fate. Ah me! silent,
Abandoned stand paternal walls
Bereft of sons; always, always at my side
Is Melancholy, sacred to the heart of poets,
Sublime mother of images born
Deep within the breast. Unknown, I am
Virgin still upon the Alps; the age of song
Has barely risen within me. One day I shall be
The Alps' noble bard, and noble verses from my lyre
Heroes shall hear: only to arouse pity
Now sing I, an unknown maiden
Dwelling among wild mountains.

*Savoy was annexed by France in 1792 and the Piedmont region was invaded in 1793.
Two of Roero's brothers were killed in the war.

IL DOLORE

Io vo' chiamando invan le rime e i versi,
Dolce conforto a' miei lunghi martìri;
Non sa l'anima mia se non dolersi,
E si disface in lagrime e sospiri;
Lassa! Dal primo dì che gli occhi apersi
Stella non è che a me benigna giri,
Sì che per molta doglia è la mia vita
Languida e secca in su l'età fiorita!

Solea talvolta, quando il chiaro sole
Volge a l'occaso le infiammate rote,
A' monti ed a le selve oscure e sole
Accomandar le mie povere note,
E al suon de le mestissime parole
Rigar di care lacrime le gote;
Così piangendo, alleviïar sentia
Il grave fascio d'ogni pena mia.

Or, quando sorge la pietosa Luna
A innamorar di sue bellezze il cielo,
Maladico le stelle ad una ad una,
E il dì che venni a provar caldo e gelo,
Maladico ogni fior che a l'aria bruna
Dolcemente riposa in su lo stelo,
Maladico ogni cosa ovunque io movo,
Che dorme in pace, ed io pace non trovo.

MARIA GUACCI NOBILE   (1808–1848)

SUFFERING

To invoke rhymes and verse in vain I try,
For soothing comfort in my long torment;
My soul can nothing but its fate lament
And wastes itself in tears and sighs.
Alas! ever since the opening of my eyes
There's been no star whose favor on me bent,
So that through painful suffering my life,
Though now in flower, drooping is and dry.

Sometimes when the shining sun
Turned his fiery wheels towards the West,
I used with my poor verses to address
The mountains and the woods, dark and lone,
And, on hearing words of deepest sadness,
Furrowed my cheeks with precious tears;
By this weeping, I felt made less
The heavy burden of my whole distress.

Now, at the rising of the pitying moon
Who makes the heavens love her beauties fair,
I curse the stars, one by one,
And the day when I came to feel heat and cold;
I curse each flower that in the darkening air
Gently rests upon its stalk;
I curse everything, everywhere I walk,
That sleeps in peace while I no peace do find.

da *I CIELI*

[...] Ali possenti ha il cor;—per man mi prendi:
Verrà seguace al vol dell'alto ingegno
Questo che m'arde del saver desio,
Questo che sì mi vince amor del vero.
Parlami il tuo linguaggio! Oh i rapimenti
D'un pensier che s'affaccia all'infinito,
Oh l'estasi d'un cor che vi s'immerge
È spettacol celeste, e Tu 'l vedrai!
Vedrai l'anima mia rifletter lieta
Quell'intimo gioir che ad ogni novo
Conoscimento l'intelletto irraggia,
Ed è un lieve quaggiù pegno di quello
Che in sen degl'Immortali eternamente
Piove il fulgor dell'Increato Lume.—

   Ecco, Tu la vicenda a me riveli
D'immutevoli leggi; ecco, io comprendo
L'armonia de' portenti, ove il pensiero
Spinsi altra volta invan.—Arcane forze
Penetrar veggo ogni atomo e dar vita
A quanto esiste. La medesma possa,
Che tragge al suolo la piovente goccia,
L'onda vi trae del Nïagàra; innalza
Del mar le spume al lunar disco incontro;
I satelliti lega ai lor pianeti,
Ed i pianeti al Sol, e ad altri Soli
Questo che su noi splende; e un magistero,
·In numero ammirando ed in misura,
Tutte regge e contien le gravitanti
Moli da quella possa affaticate. [...]

CATERINA BON BRENZONI   (1813–1856)

from *THE HEAVENS*

[. . .] The heart has powerful wings;—take me by the hand:
Following the flight of high intelligence will come
This desire for knowledge that burns within me,
This love of truth that overpowers me so.
Speak to me your language! Oh, the raptures
Of a thought that turns towards the infinite,
Oh, the ecstasy of a heart immersed in it
Is a heavenly sight, and you shall witness it!
You shall witness my joyful soul reflect
That intimate delight that irradiates
The intellect at each new knowledge
And is but a small presage in this world of that
Which rains forever on the bosom of the Immortals
The brilliance of Uncreated Light.

   Behold, to me you disclose the workings
Of immutable laws; behold, I comprehend
The harmony of portents where at other times
I urged my thought in vain. I see mysterious
Forces penetrate every atom and give life
To all existence. The same power
That draws to the earth the drop of rain
Also draws Niagara's flood; it raises
The sea's spray to meet the lunar disc;
It binds the planets to the Sun, and to other Suns
Ours that shines on us; and a masterly skill
Admirable in quantity and scope
Regulates and holds in check all the
Gravitating masses worked on by that power. [. . .]

ALLA MADRE

Oh, forse dubbio in te, forse tormento
Destava, o madre, questo cor di foco;
Questo che audace, irrequïeto sento;

Questo che in ogni tempo, in ogni loco
S'agita e freme, sicché pace invano
Invan quiete a tanti affetti invoco?

Oh, come è procelloso, oh, come è strano
Tanto crudel tumulto in sì verd'anni!
Qual è simile al mio, qual petto umano?

Benché aperta cagion non ho d'affanni,
Esser lieta non so, né so lagnarmi
Per non far tuoi dell'egra mente i danni.

Deh, spera, madre mia! Saprò ispirarmi
Ne' tuoi detti, saprò vincer me stessa,
Saprò la gloria ritentar de' carmi

E ogni cosa obliar che sì m'ha oppressa.

IL TARLO

Due anni si compiro, e in questa stanza,
Entro codesto armario per più mesi,
Con feroce costanza,
O vecchio tarlo, rodere t'intesi;
Riedo, e vivente anco ti trovo e ascoso
Nel mobile corroso,
Da cui strapparti tenterebbe invano
Chi ridur nol volesse a brano a brano.

Spesso tra veglie amare
Ascoltando il tuo metro
Sì monotono e tetro,
Ad un povero cor soglio pensare
Ove pur penetrava un tarlo audace
Che senza tregua roderlo si piace.

GIUSEPPINA TURRISI COLONNA   (1822–1848)

TO MY MOTHER

Oh, perhaps your doubt, perhaps anxiety
Were roused, oh mother, by this fiery heart;
This rash and restless heart I feel in me;

This heart that always and in every part
Is moved and trembles, so that on peace vainly,
vainly on calm I call for so much passion?

Oh how turbulent, oh how strange
is such cruel torment at such tender age!
What like mine, what human breast like mine?

Though patent cause for trouble I have none,
Happy I cannot be, nor can I complain
Lest I make yours this sick mind's pain.

Oh mother mine, take hope! Inspired I'll be
by your own words, myself I'll overcome,
I shall aspire anew to poetry's fame

And every thing forget that cast me down.

ERMINIA FUA FUSINATO   (1834–1876)

THE WOODWORM

Two full years went by, and in this room
For many months inside that cupboard
With savage perseverance,
I heard you gnaw, old worm.
I return and find you still alive, unseen
Within the riddled furniture,
Whence to dislodge you one could try in vain,
Not wanting to reduce it piece by piece.

Often in bitter sleepless hours,
Listening to your rhythm
So monotonous and sad,
I think continually of an unhappy heart
Wherein, too, a bold worm penetrated
And there is pleased to gnaw incessantly.

Sol mentre ad ogni orecchio manifesto
Rendi il tuo lavorìo,
Non conosce che Dio
Quanto l'altro a quel cor torni funesto:
Di fuori il riso e la vernice, e ognora
Di dentro il tarlo e legno e cor divora:

    Allor che l'opra eccede,
Dal fondo dell'armario una leggiera
Tritura uscir si vede;
Quando l'ambascia al cor scende più fiera,
Sopra freddo guancial cadon le stille
Di due stanche pupille.

    Questi celati roditori e lenti
Così proseguon nello strano accordo:
Dall'insensibil legno escon lamenti,
E tace il core o il suo lamento è sordo.
Lì materia consuma e qui la vita
Il tarlo parassita,
E quasi al par del legno si dissolve
Il cor che pace avrà col legno in polve.

DI SERA

Ed eccomi qui sola, a udir ancora
il lieve brontolìo de' tizzi ardenti;
eccomi ad aspettarlo: è uscito or ora
canticchiando, col sigaro tra i denti.

Gravi faccende lo chiamavan fuora:
gli amici al giuoco de le carte intenti,
od un soprano che di vezzi infiora
d'una storpiata melodia gli accenti.

E per questo riman da me diviso
fin che la mezzanotte o il tocco suona
a l'orologio d'una chiesa accanto.

Poi torna allegro, m'accarezza il viso,
e mi domanda se son stata buona,
senza nemmeno sospettar che ho pianto.

Only, while evident to every ear
You make your work,
No one knows but God
What doom the other worm brings to that dismal heart.
Outside, the smile, the varnish, and all the while
Inside, the worm consumes both wood and heart:

When the work has gone too far,
Then from the cupboard's depths a powdery dust
Drifts down;
When the pain gnaws more harshly at the heart
Upon the cold pillow the drops fall
From two weary eyes.

These gnawing things, hidden and slow,
Thus proceed together in strange accord;
From the insensible wood laments come forth,
While the heart is silent, its lament dulled.
There matter and here life
The parasitic worm consumes,
And almost equally with the wood dissolves
The heart that, like the wood, will have peace in dust.

LA CONTESSA LARA   (1849–1896)

IN THE EVENING

And here am I alone, still listening
to the soft grumbling of burning coals;
here am I waiting for him: he left just now
humming a tune, a cigar between his teeth.

Serious business summons him forth:
friends, intent on playing a game of cards,
or a soprano who loves to embellish
the phrases of a mangled melody.

This is why he stays away from me
until midnight or until the hour of one strikes
in the clock of a church nearby.

Then he gaily returns, strokes my face,
and asks me if I have been good,
without ever suspecting that I have wept.

L'ULTIMO CANTO DI SAFFO

Mare, l'ultimo canto
È per te; dico a te l'ultima mia
Parola disperata senza pianto,
Mare infinito come il mio dolore.
Questo mio folle amore
E l'impeto e la sete,
Furono vani; ed io
Inclamidata nell'orgoglio mio,
Serena in vista e non compresa mai,
Per la vita passai
Come un'ignota per ignoto lido,
Mordendo le mie mani
A contenere il grido.

Mare, son tua; m'abbraccia,
Mi stringi e chiudi come chiuso e stretto
Sull'adorato petto
Questo mio corpo non fu mai. L'ardente
Mia carne è tua; con mille spire avvinta
Sia da te, pòsi in te, giù finalmente
Cada, placata e vinta
Dal tuo bacio possente.

VITTORIA AGANOOR POMPILI   (1855–1910)

SAPPHO'S LAST SONG

Sea, the last song
Is for you: to you I speak my last
Hopeless word, without tears,
Sea infinite as my suffering.
This mad love of mine
And the vehemence and the thirst
Were in vain; and I,
Enclosed in the chlamys of my pride,
Serene in appearance and never understood,
Passed through life
As an unknown woman on an unknown shore,
Biting my hands
To contain my scream.

Sea, I am yours; embrace me,
Clasp me and enfold me as enfolded and clasped
On the beloved's breast
This body of mine has never been. My burning
Flesh is yours; with a thousand coils let it be
Bound by you, let it rest in you, down at last
Let it sink, calmed and conquered
By your mighty kiss.

EGO

O Mondo, vecchia guardia doganale,
Farai l'obbligo tuo da buon cristiano:
Giusta e severa sia la tua condanna,
Chè non ti voglio dar la buona mano!

Sono in contravvenzione, o Mondo astuto.
Volea truffarti con la merce mia:
Non è tabacco, sigari o liquori,
Nulla di spiritoso: è poesia!

Il Mondo ha spalancato i suoi mille occhi,
E "Chi sei tu?" mi grida: e "cosa fai?
Dimmi la fede tua, l'età, la patria,
Che cerchi, donde vieni e dove vai!"

—Del mio paese chiedi? Io ti rispondo:
Non ho paese: è mia tutta la terra!
La patria mia qual'è? Mamma è tedesca,
Babbo italiano, io nacqui in Inghilterra.

E quale la mia fede? Io vado a messa;
La musica mi edifica e ricrea:
Ma sono battezzata protestante.
Di nome e di profilo sono ebrea.

Chiedi dell'età mia? Quasi ho vent'anni.
E quale la mia meta? Ancor l'ignoro.
Che cerco? Nulla. Attendo il mio destino,
E rido e canto e piango e m'innamoro.

E cielo e terra, paradiso e inferno
Sfioro coll' ali della fantasia!
Non chieder altro.—Impetuosa e strana
Per nuove vie fugge la vita mia.

Fugge nel buio e crede nella luce.
L'anima fiduciosa e calma e forte
Ispirata mi guida. A che?—*Si vive*.
Quel gran problema scioglierà la morte.

ANNIE VIVANTI (1868–1942)

EGO

O world, you old customs officer,
You will do your duty like a good Christian:
May your sentence be just and stern,
For I've no wish to grease your palm.

I am subject to a fine, O wily world.
I tried to cheat you over my merchandise:
It is not tobacco, cigars or liquor,
Nothing spirited: it is poetry!

The world has opened wide its thousand eyes
And shouts: "Who are you? What do you do?
Tell me your faith, your age, your country,
What you seek, whence you came and whither you go!"

—You ask about my country? I reply:
I have no country: the whole earth is mine!
What is my fatherland? Mama is German,
Papa Italian, I was born in England.

And what is my faith? I go to Mass:
The music uplifts and delights me.
I was baptized a Protestant.
My name and profile are Jewish.

You ask my age? I'm almost twenty.
And what is my goal? I don't know yet.
What do I seek? Nothing. I await my destiny
And laugh and sing and weep and fall in love.

And over heaven and earth, paradise and hell,
I skim with wings of fantasy!
Nothing else I ask.—Impetuous and strange,
My life flies along new ways.

It flies in the dark and believes in the light.
My soul, faithful and calm and strong
Leads me inspired. To what?—*We live*.
That great problem death will resolve.

SFIDA

O grasso mondo di borghesi astuti
di calcoli nudrito e di polpette,
mondo di milionari ben pasciuti
                e di bimbe civette;

o mondo di clorotiche donnine
che vanno a messa per guardar l'amante,
o mondo d'adulterii e di rapine
                e di speranze infrante;

e sei tu dunque, tu, mondo bugiardo,
che vuoi celarmi il sol degl'ideali,
e sei tu dunque, tu, pigmeo codardo,
                che vuoi tarparmi l'ali? . . .

Tu strisci, io volo; tu sbadigli, io canto:
tu menti e pungi e mordi, io ti disprezzo:
dell'estro arride a me l'aurato incanto,
                tu t'affondi nel lezzo.

O grasso mondo d'oche e di serpenti,
mondo vigliacco, che tu sia dannato!
Fiso lo sguardo negli astri fulgenti,
                io movo incontro al fato:

sitibonda di luce, inerme e sola,
movo.—E più tu ristai, scettico e gretto,
più d'amor la fatidica parola
                mi prorompe dal petto! . . .

Va, grasso mondo, va per l'aer perso
di prostitute e di denari in traccia:
io, con la frusta del bollente verso,
                ti sferzo in su la faccia.

ADA NEGRI   (1870–1945)

CHALLENGE

Oh fat world of crafty bourgeois
fed with calculations and croquettes,
world of well-fattened millionaires
                    and young coquettes;

oh world of tiny anemic women
who go to Mass to see their lovers,
oh world of adulteries and plunder
                    and hopes in tatters;

you lying world, is it you then
who wants to hide the sun of ideals from me?
you pygmy coward, is it you then
                    who wants to clip my wings?...

You crawl, I soar; you yawn, I sing;
you lie and needle and bite, you I scorn:
on me smiles the gold charm of imagining,
                    you in filth sink down.

Oh fat world of geese and snakes,
dastardly world, may you be damned!
I fix my sight on the brilliant stars,
                    I go to meet my fate:

thirsting for light, unarmed and alone,
I move.—And the more you, skeptical and narrow-minded, desist,
the more the prophetic word of love
                    bursts from my breast!...

Be off, fat world, be off through air darkling
with prostitutes, and hot on money's trace;
I, with whip of seething verse,
                    shall strike you in the face.

SON TANTO BRAVA

Son tanto brava lungo il giorno.
Comprendo, accetto, non piango.
Quasi imparo ad aver orgoglio quasi fossi un uomo.
Ma, al primo brivido di viola in cielo
ogni diurno sostegno dispare.
Tu mi sospiri lontano: "Sera, sera dolce e mia!"
Sembrami d'aver fra le dita la stanchezza di tutta la terra.
Non son piú che sguardo, sguardo sperduto, e vene.

UNA NOTTE IN CARCERE

Pace era nella cella
e sconfinava di là dalle sbarre di ferro
sovra la notte di gran pioggia e sul mondo,
pace m'avvolse,
la cella era simile ad una tomba.
Gelo, sentor di muffa, oscillante ombra.
Silenzio umano immenso, al canto della pioggia.
Ogni prigioniera forse dormiva, e ogni dolore.

Oh notte, oh morte, oh mia libertà!

Giaceva la mia libertà
quella notte come in una tomba,
il bel mito giaceva
per amor del quale ho vissuto ardendo.
Lungi le spiagge le rose le selve.
E creatura nessuna in pena per me,
nessuno nella notte ad attendermi lungi.
Nuda anima, quanta pace!
Le piú azzurre sponde,
vastità lucenti, sinfonie di stelle,
serene alla memoria sbocciavano.

Pure, gli uomini e la lor giustizia
potevano, poveri uomini, ne l'errore persistere,
poteva l'alba non riportarmi libertà...
Sovra la notte di gran pioggia e sul mondo,
di là dalle sbarre di ferro,
l'errore forse infieriva...

SIBILLA ALERAMO   (1876–1960)

I AM SO GOOD

I am so good all day long.
I understand, I accept, I do not weep.
I almost learn to be proud as if I were a man.
But, at the first quiver of violet in the sky
all daytime strength vanishes.
Far off you sigh to me: "Evening, evening sweet and mine!"
Between my fingers I seem to hold the weariness of the whole world.
I am nothing more than a look, a lost look, and veins.

A NIGHT IN PRISON

There was peace in the cell
and it escaped beyond the iron bars
over the night of great rain and onto the world,
peace enveloped me,
the cell was like a tomb.
Cold, smell of mould, wavering darkness.
Immense human silence, to the song of the rain.
Every prisoner slept perhaps, and every pain.

Oh night, oh death, oh my freedom!

My freedom was in abeyance
that night as if in a tomb,
the fine myth was in abeyance
for the love of which I have lived aflame.
Far away the beaches the roses the woods.
And no creature in anguish for me,
nobody in the night waiting for me far away.
Naked soul, how deep a peace!
The bluest shores,
shining immensities, symphonies of stars,
were blossoming serene in my memory.

And yet, men and their justice
could, poor men, persist in their error,
the dawn might not restore my liberty...
Over the night of great rain and onto the world,
beyond the iron bars,
the error was perhaps raging...

Nella cella tutta ombra
una nuda certezza allora
in me sentii,
meravigliosamente
in me assolta sentii la vita intera,
folta di sogni, passionata ed aspra,
ogni giorno espiata,
vita d'opere e di lacrime,
e il cielo s'apriva ad archi sorridenti,
di quando in quando, fuggitivi!

Meraviglia limpida, trasparente mistero,
nella notte di prigionia
trovarsi lieve, sí, alata come non mai,
nella cella simile ad una tomba...

Cosí forse in una risurrezione confiderò
quando morta giacerò
a fior di terra o in fondo al mare?

SÍ ALLA TERRA

Tanto splende nella luce di certi mattini
con le sue rose e con i suoi cipressi
la Terra o col suo grano e i suoi ulivi,

tanto di repente splende all'anima
e la isola e di ogni cosa la smemora
s'anche un attimo prima l'anima
dolorava a sangue o amara meditava,

tanto splende nella luce di certi mattini
la Terra e in suo silenzio si palesa,
meravigliosa zolla rotolante dai cieli,
e bella in sua tragica solitudine tanto ride,

che l'anima, pur non interrogata,
"Sí" risponde, "Sí" alla Terra,
alla indifferente Terra "Sí,"

s'anche dovessero fra un attimo i cieli
oscurarsi e le rose e i cipressi,
o piú grave farsi la fatica del vivere
e piú eroico ancora il respiro,

"Sí" soggiogata risponde l'anima alla Terra.
tanto splende nella luce di certi mattini
bella sovra ogni cosa e speranza umana.

In the cell's utter darkness
a naked certainty
I then felt within me,
marvelously
I felt the whole of life absolved in me,
life teeming with dreams, life passionate and harsh,
life expiated each day,
life of work and tears,
and from time to time the sky opened
to smiling fleeting rainbows!

Limpid marvel, transparent mystery,
in the night of imprisonment
to find oneself light, yes, winged as never before,
in the tomb-like cell...

And so shall I perhaps rely on a resurrection
when I lie dead
on the face of the earth or at the bottom of the sea?

YES TO THE EARTH

So shines the Earth in certain mornings' light
with its roses and cypresses
or with its grain and its olives,

so suddenly does it shine on the soul
and isolates it and makes it forget everything
even if an instant earlier the soul
was suffering to the quick or meditating, bitter,

so shines the Earth in certain mornings' light
and in its silence reveals itself,
a marvelous lump spinning from the skies,
and, beautiful in its tragic solitude, so laughs

that the soul, although not asked,
answers, "Yes," "Yes," to the Earth,
to the indifferent Earth "Yes,"

even if in an instant the skies and the roses
and the cypresses should turn dark,
or the labor of living be made more burdensome
and breathing yet more heroic,

"Yes," the subjugated soul answers the Earth,
so does it shine in certain mornings' light,
beautiful over all things and human hope.

LA MIA VOCE

La mia voce non ha rombo di mare
o d'echi alti tra fughe di colonne:
ma il susurro che par fruscìo di gonne
con cui si narran feminili gare.

Io non volli cantar, volli parlare,
e dir cose di me, di tante donne
cui molti desideri urgon l'insonne
cuore e lascian con labbra un poco amare.

E amara è pur la mia voce talvolta,
quasi vi tremi un riso d'ironia,
più pungente a chi parla che a chi ascolta.

Come quando a un'amica si confida
qualche segreto di malinconia
e si ha paura ch'ella ne sorrida.

IL DESTINO

La donna, con il volto fra le mani,
nell'ombra di sua gran chioma raccolto,
pensa:—Avrò ancora il mio nome e il mio volto
fra un anno, oppur fra dieci anni, o domani?

Darò la carne quasi fatta a brani
a un figlio ancor nel suo mister sepolto,
o isterilita, l'offrirò allo stolto
desìo, all'arsura de' piaceri insani?

Fragile donna, ella non sa, non vuole,
non dispera: l'ignoto è un grande peso
sul suo piccolo cuor che non si duole.

È il suo destino orribilmente bello,
sempre a un filo esilissimo sospeso:
a un filo tenue come un suo capello.

AMALIA GUGLIELMINETTI   (1881–1941)

MY VOICE

My voice has not the roar of the sea
or of deep echoes through flights of columns:
but the whisper that seems the rustle of skirts
with which feminine rivalries are told.

I did not want to sing, I wanted to speak,
and tell about myself, about so many women
whose numerous desires arouse their sleepless
hearts and leave them with slightly bitter lips.

And bitter too is my voice at times,
a smile of irony almost quivers in it,
more pungent to the speaker than to the listener.

As when we confide in a friend
some melancholy secret
and are afraid that she will smile at it.

DESTINY

The woman, her face between her hands,
nestled in the shadow of her great mane,
thinks: "Shall I still have my name and my face
in a year's time, or in ten years, or tomorrow?

Shall I give my flesh torn almost to pieces
to a son still entombed in his mystery,
or, rendered barren, shall I offer it to foolish
desire, to the burning of mad pleasures?"

Fragile woman, she neither knows, nor wishes,
nor despairs: the unknown is a huge weight
on her little, uncomplaining heart.

Her destiny is terribly beautiful,
always suspended on the thinnest thread:
a thread as fine as one of her hairs.

IL LAMENTO DELLA SPOSA

Aveo le fibbie belle,
aveo de be' vestiti,
ora mi so' spariti in su i' momento

l'orologio d'argento
e' ci tenevo appesa
una bella catenina ciondoloni;

io gli feci i calzoni,
calzette e sottoveste
e giubba delle feste e un be' cappello;

credeva d'esse bello
con tutto i' suo' ballare,
a me tocca stentare, poverina!

la sera e la mattina
mi trovo disperata,
ho fatto la frittata, e me credete,

fui messa nella rete
dalla mi' zia Simona
e dalla baccellona della Nena;

preso che l'ebbi appena,
questo tristo marito,
mangiare i' pan pentito a me conviene;

credevo di stà bene
e pe' fammi dispetto
e' m'ha venduto i' letto e i' cassettone.

Ragazze belle e bone,
da me tutte imparate,
zitelle e maritate, a avé giudizio:

s'entra in un precipizio
appena fatte spose;
e so dell'altre cose e 'un le vò dire;

con questo vò finire
e non vò andà più 'n là:
polenta e baccalà l'è un boccon bono.

ANONYMOUS POPULAR SONGS
(LATE NINETEENTH AND EARLY TWENTIETH CENTURIES)

THE HOUSEWIFE'S LAMENT

I used to have fine buckles
I used to have fine clothes,
now they have vanished all in a flash

my silver timepiece
and hanging with it
I had a fine chain dangling;

for him I made pants,
some socks and undershirts
a holiday jacket and a fine hat;

he thought it was great
to go dance with his friends,
I'm on my beam-ends, misery my share!

I'm in despair
all nights and mornings,
I made a mess of things, you better believe it,

I was trapped in the net
by my aunt Simona
and by that great ninny who is called Nena;

I had barely taken
this wretch of a husband
when I had to eat the bread of repentance;

I was well off I thought
when just to spite me
he sold my bed from me, my hope chest as well.

You good and pretty girls,
learn from me all of you,
maids and matrons too, take grandma's advice:

we go to our downfall
as soon as we're brides;
and I know other things I'd like to tell;

but with this I'll finish
and then go no further:
polenta and codfish make a good mouthful.

LA MALCONTENTA

Dirindina la malcontenta,
babbo gode e mamma stenta,

babbo va all'osteria,
mamma tribola tuttavia;

babbo mangia l'erbe cotte,
mamma tribola giorno e notte;

babbo mangia e beve i' vino,
mamma tribola co i' cittino;

babbo mangia li fagioli,
mamma tribola coi figlioli;

babbo mangia 'l baccalà,
mamma tribola a tutt'andà;

babbo mangia le polpette,
mamma fa delle crocette.

Dirindina la malcontenta,
babbo gode e mamma stenta...

POVERE FILANDINE

Povere filandine,
desfortunàe che semo,
la paga che ciapemo
li ne la vol magnar.

Ghe ne ciapemo trenta,
li ne magna quaranta,
al zioba li ne la canta,
al sabo li ne la tien.

Povere filandine,
desfortunàe che semo,
la paga che ciapemo
li ne la vol magnar.

Povere filandine,
levemo su a bonora,
ciapemo una malora
par mèso franco al dì.

THE DISCONTENTED WOMAN

Dirindina the discontented,
papa has fun and mama's tormented,

papa to the tavern goes his way,
mama worries anyway;

papa eats boiled dandelions,
mama worries all the time;

papa eats and drinks his wine,
mama worries for every dime;

papa eats up his fagioli,
mama over the children worries;

papa eats the codfish up,
mama worries like all get out;

papa finishes the meatballs off,
mama makes little signs of the cross.

Dirindina the discontented,
papa has fun and mama's tormented...

SONG OF THE VENETIAN SILK-SPINNERS

Poor silk-spinners,
we are so wretched,
the pay that we get
they eat it back off us.

For we get thirty,
of it they eat forty,
on Thursday they crow about it,
on Saturday they withhold it.

Poor silk-spinners,
we are so wretched,
the pay that we get
they eat it back off us.

Poor silk-spinners,
we get up so early,
killing ourselves
for half a lira a day.

E anche 'l caposala
che no xe bon da gnente,
ghe vegna un asidente
su la punta del cor.

Povere filandine...

O CARA MAMMA, VIENIMI INCONTRA

O cara mamma, vienimi incontra,
che ho tante cose da raccontare
che nel parlare mi fan tremare
la brutta vita che ho passà.

La brutta vita che ho passato
là sul trapianto e nella monda;
la mia bella faccia rotonda
come prima non la vedrai più.

Alla mattina quei moscerini
che ci succhiavano tutto quel sangue
e a mezzogiorno quel brutto sole
che ci faceva abbrustolir.

A mezzogiorno fagioli e riso
e alla sera riso e fagioli
e quel pane non naturale
che l'appetito ci fa mancar.

E alle nove la ritirata
e alle dieci c'è l'ispezione,
l'ispezione del padrone:
tutte in branda a riposar.

E LA MI' MAMMA LA ME LO DICEVA

E la mi' mamma la me lo diceva:
piglià marito nun farà ma' bene;
andare a letto a lume della luna,
il piatto in grembio e il piede sulla cuna.

Quando ti credi d'andartene a dormire,
piglialo l'ago e metteti a cucire,
quando ti credi d'andartene a letto
prendi il bambino e mettetelo al petto.

And the foreman too
who's a good for nothing,
may an accident befall him
on the point of his heart.

Poor silk-spinners...

SONG OF THE RICE WORKERS

Oh mama dear, come and meet me,
for I've so many things to tell you
that talking of them makes me tremble
the awful life that I've been leading.

The awful life that I've been leading
there, weeding and transplanting;
you'll no longer see my face
round and pretty, as it used to be.

In the morning those mosquitoes
that would suck our blood
and at noon that awful sun
that would scorch and burn us.

At noon beans and rice
in the evening rice and beans
and that artificial bread
that takes away our appetite.

And at nine o'clock the washroom
and at ten o'clock inspection,
inspection by the boss:
all of us to rest on folding cots.

AND MY MAMA USED TO TELL ME

And my mama used to tell me:
a husband doesn't help you any;
you go to bed by the light of the moon,
your foot on the cradle, the dish in your apron.

When you think of going to sleep,
you pick up your needle and then start sewing,
when you think about getting some rest
you pick up the baby and give him your breast.

LA PORTA CHE SI CHIUDE

Tu lo vedi, sorella: io sono stanca—
come il pilastro d'un cancello angusto
diga nel tempo all'irruente fuga
d'una folla rinchiusa.

Oh, le parole prigioniere
che battono battono
furiosamente
alla porta dell'anima
e la porta dell'anima
che a palmo a palmo
spietatamente
si chiude!

Ed ogni giorno il varco si stringe
ed ogni giorno l'assalto è più duro.

E l'ultimo giorno—
io lo so—
l'ultimo giorno,
quando un'unica lama di luce
pioverà dall'estremo spiraglio
dentro la tenebra,
allora sarà l'urto tremendo,
l'urlo mortale
delle parole non nate
verso l'ultimo sogno di sole.

E poi,
dietro la porta per sempre chiusa,
sarà la notte intera,
la frescura,
il silenzio.

E poi, con le labbra serrate,
con gli occhi aperti
sull'arcano cielo dell'ombra,
sarà
—tu lo sai—
la pace.

ANTONIA POZZI (1912–1938)

THE CLOSING DOOR

As you see, sister, I am weary—
like the gate post of a narrow wicket
barrier against the erupting flight
of a pent-up mob.

Oh, the prisoner words
that are pounding, pounding
angrily
at the door of the soul
and the door of the soul
that little by little
is mercilessly
closing!

And every day the passageway narrows
and every day the attack is heavier.

And the final day—
I know—
the final day,
when a single blade of light
falls from the furthest peephole
in the darkness,
then the shock will be tremendous,
the mortal howl
of unborn words
toward the final dream of sunlight.

And then,
behind the door closed forever,
will be total night,
cold air,
silence.

And then, with locked lips,
with open eyes
under the shadow's mysterious sky,
will be
—as you know—
peace.

PRESAGIO

Esita l'ultima luce
fra le dita congiunte dei pioppi—
l'ombra trema di freddo e d'attesa
dietro di noi
e lenta muove intorno le braccia
per farci piú soli.

Cade l'ultima luce
sulle chiome dei tigli—
in cielo le dita dei pioppi
s'inanellano di stelle.

Qualcosa dal cielo discende
verso l'ombra che trema—
qualcosa passa
nella tenebra nostra
come un biancore—
forse qualcosa che ancora non è—
forse qualcuno che sarà
domani—
forse una creatura
del nostro pianto.

LETTERA IN PRESENTE E PASSATO PROSSIMO

Tu lo sai come sono certe volte.
Ho pregato e pregato la mia saggia
ironia di salvarmi
di ridere alquanto di me.
E invece sto in ascolto tutto il tempo
del raffio che mi scarna
d'una mano di ferro che si aggrappa.
Ti dirò: sono troppo civile
per urlare, per dire le cose
abbandonatamente. Nessuna
catarsi, tu lo vedi,
per una condizionata
a decenza di belle maniere.

PREMONITION

The last light lingers
between the linked fingers of the poplars—
the shadow quivers with cold and expectancy
behind us
and slowly moves around our arms
to make us more alone.

The last light falls
on the long hair of the lindens—
in the sky the fingers of the poplars
put on their rings of stars.

Something comes down from the sky
towards the quivering shadow—
Something passes
in our darkness
like a whiteness—
perhaps something that is not yet—
perhaps someone who will be
tomorrow—
perhaps a creature
of our tears.

DARIA MENICANTI (1914–)

LETTER IN THE PRESENT AND PRESENT PERFECT

You know how I am at certain times.
I have begged and begged my wise
irony to save me
to laugh at myself a little.
And instead I spend the whole time listening
for the hook that will strip me of flesh
for an iron hand that holds me fast.
I shall say to you: I am too polite
to scream, to speak out
freely with abandon. No
catharsis, as you see,
for someone conditioned
to the propriety of good manners.

Sono uscita alla pioggia. Ti ricordi:
m'è sempre piaciuto girare
col vento sotto l'acqua che vola
attaccare discorso coi randagi
lungo i viali scarlatti.
Un bimbo camminava
a guinzaglio di un'altra: mi ha toccato
sussurrando dolcissimi nonsensi.
Ho guardato alla sua tenerezza, a quel libro
bianco e intonso di lui.
Questo confronto, questo
sentirsi quaggiù per imprestito,
l'uscire tra le stelle di Natale
non è la gran soluzione.
Così sono tornata a casa a scriverti
una lettera.

MOLTE VOLTE NOVEMBRE È RITORNATO

Molte volte novembre è ritornato
Nella mia vita, e questo che oggi ha inizio
Non è il peggiore: quieto
Benché non privo di apprensione. China
Mi trova su una culla, dove l'ultima
Mia nata dorme il misterioso
Profondo sonno dell'infanzia, ancora
Ospite più che cittadina in questo
Nostro mondo per lei straniero. Sento
La dolce ondata del latte salirmi
Al seno: tenerezza
Che di sé gonfia tutte le mie fibre,
Dilata i miei confini. Qui lo stanco
Sangue si rifà puro a una segreta
Sorgente, si rifà vergine e può
Calmar la sete di vergini labbra.
Il mio corpo è strumento di miracolo
Come già fu nel dare vita. Il seno
È la collina favolosa, scorrono

I went out in the rain. You remember:
I have always liked to wander about
in the wind with the water flying
to start conversations with stray passersby
along the scarlet avenues.
A little child was walking along
in a harness held by another woman: he touched me
whispering the dearest nonsense.
I gazed at his tender love, at the
blank uncut book of himself.
This meeting, this
feeling of being down here on loan,
going out among the Christmas stars
is not the great solution.
And so I came back home to write you
a letter.

MARGHERITA GUIDACCI   (1921–)

MANY TIMES NOVEMBER HAS COME BACK

Many times November has come back
Into my life, and the one starting today
Is not the worst: peaceful
Although not lacking apprehension. It finds
Me leaning over a cradle where my last
Born daughter sleeps the mysterious
Deep sleep of infancy, still
More guest than citizen in this
World of ours so foreign to her. I feel
Within me the sweet surge of milk rising
To my breast: tenderness
That spontaneously fills my every fiber
Dilates my borders. Here the tired
Blood repurifies itself at a secret
Source, becomes virginal again and can
Quench the thirst of virgin lips.
My body is the instrument of a miracle
As it already was in giving life. My breast
Is the fabled hill, rivers

I fiumi d'abbondanza in un'età
D'oro che segnerà
Per la creatura ignara il più profondo
Alveo della memoria, a cui più tardi
Ritornerà nel sogno o nel dolore...
Per lei intatta è l'immagine; per me
Che ne sono occasione, la scolora
Già il tempo, amaramente. È forse l'ultima
Volta che ho un figlio al seno, poiché incalzano
Gli anni ad inaridire
La mia linfa. Oggi sono
Ancora un vivo albero, frusciante
Di foglie, benedetto
Di succhi, ma in cammino è la stagione
Spoglia che su di me si chiuderà.
Tanto più dolce è questa sosta, prima
Ch'io stessa sia l'autunno: pure un'ombra
Di presagio la vela e di paura.
Il passato si stende alle mie spalle
Come una lunga via. So del futuro
Solo una cosa: che difficilmente
Potrà uguagliare per me la durata
Del tempo ch'è trascorso.

UOMO

Altro da me in tutto...maschio, estraneo,
altra carne, altro cuore, altra mente,
pure, il mio stesso corpo prolungato,
la voce che si sdoppia, e mi continua:
ciò che si oppone, e ciò che mi compone
come un discorso teso, mai concluso
o l'altro occhio: il raggio che converge
al rilievo, allo scatto delle cose—
mio necessario opposto, crudele meraviglia
è amare te: godere di due vite
in questa sola, avere doppia morte.

Of plenty are flowing in a golden
Age that will mark
For the unwitting child memory's
Deepest channel, to which she later
Will return in dream or sorrow...
For her the image is intact; for me
Who has occasioned it, time discolors
It already, bitterly. It may be the last
Time I have a baby at my breast, for the years
Press on to parch
My lymph. Today I am
Still a living tree, rustling
With leaves, blessed
With sap, but approaching is the barren
Season which will engulf me.
This respite is that much the sweeter, before
I myself am autumn: even so a shadow
Of foreboding hangs over it—and of fear.
The past stretches behind my shoulders
Like a long road. Of the future I know
One thing only: that it can hardly
Afford me time
Equal to that already spent.

ARMANDA GUIDUCCI   (1923–)

MAN

Different from me entirely: male, foreign,
different flesh, different heart, different mind,
and yet my own body in extension,
my voice that doubles itself and continues me:
that which opposes, and that which composes me
like a drawn out discourse, never ended,
or the other eye: the beam that converges
on the focal point, at the click of things—
my necessary opposite, a cruel marvel
it is to love you: to enjoy two lives
in this one, to have double death.

PARITÀ

Ed ora tu mi dici (è la tua voce,
la voce che è l'affetto mosso in suono),
con la tua voce calda tu mi dici
(la voce dei momenti più preziosi,
la voce che mi lega in mille nodi),
con quella lunga voce tu mi dici:
"Non sono ora, e non fui mai felice,
nonostante te, completamente."

Tu chiedi l'uomo in me: che io capisca,
ad onta di me stessa...e disconosca
la mia mitica forza: essere donna
—orgoglio ch'è più antico del pensiero.

Posso capirti, distratto in altre vite
e progetti di vita. Se neghi me,
tu ti rinventi sulla carta bianca.
Io, suggerisco un'unica versione.
Io sono ciò che hai. E, se mai gioia,
—di un'esistenza sola, limitata.
Forse, ogni donna è immagine di morte,
senza saperlo, più stretto abbracci un uomo.

Dunque, ho compreso te—e sono esclusa.
Che crollo costa, la parità con l'uomo.

LA CANZONE DEL MARTELLO

Forza, mi dicevo, fatti forza.
Il martello è fatto per scolpire
dalla massa brutale. E fui martello.
Scolpii forme ai giorni
all'amorfa noia quotidiana
accarezzando le pietre in cerca d'anima
con accanimento femminile
come si crea un bambino
con slancio
d'ogni minuto plasmato.
Ribadivo le pieghe delle notti—
si rimbocca cosí una coperta
su chi si ama.

EQUALITY

And now you tell me (it's your voice,
the voice which is affection turned to sound),
with your warm voice you tell me
(the voice of our most precious moments,
the voice that ties me in a thousand knots),
with that slow voice you tell me:
"I am not now, nor have I ever been happy,
in spite of you, completely."

You ask the man in me: to understand,
in spite of myself... and to disclaim
my mythical strength: being a woman
—a pride more ancient than thought.

I can understand you, diverted into other lives
and projects of life. If you renounce me
you can redesign yourself on blank paper.
I, I represent a single version.
I am what you have. And even if there is sometimes joy,
I am limited to one existence only.
Perhaps every woman is death's image,
without knowing it, the more strongly she embraces a man.

And so I have understood you—and am shut out.
What a price to pay for equality with man.

SONG OF THE HAMMER

Courage, I told myself, gather courage.
The hammer is made for sculpting
from the brute mass. And I was a hammer.
I sculpted forms out of the days
out of the amorphous everyday boredom
caressing the stones in search of soul
with feminine tenacity
as a child is created
with impetus
molded every minute.
I riveted the folds of nights—
just as a blanket is folded
over a loved one.

Legavo gli interstizi
con salde teste di chiodi.
Scommettevo speranze
come fossero certezze.

Ho creduto
nella forza quotidiana dell'amore
creativamente
da donna
nel senso di una fiera civiltà
dell'introversione femminile
calata da attese,
da stanze alte, remote.

Ho fatto giorni, bambini,
sfamato corpi e minuti d'amore,
sgorgato latte dai seni e dai bricchi
sulle soglie insistenti dei mattini.
Mi sono spaccata come una melograna
sui miei figli abortiti e i non nati.
Ho tentato
di trasformare in durata un incontro,
di abbracciare nell'uomo
la sua diversità.

Ma come ora mi torna nemico
ciò che ho abbracciato
e i giorni creati si disfanno
e sui bricchi i mattini
e i minuti creduti
e dalla passione è nata l'offesa
l'inimicizia, l'egoismo sessuale
e sulla tentata costruzione

impietosi
i colpi del piccone.

Quanta fatica per crearsi un corpo,
risvegliarne, nel proprio, uno vero.
E ora che ne possiedo uno, e l'uomo
ad altezza di donna è modellato in me
nelle curve saldate di una crescita,

ora il corpo è maturo invecchia muore.

I linked the interstices
with solid heads of nails.
I gambled hopes
as though they were certainties.

I have believed
in the everyday strength of love
creatively
as a woman
in the heart of a fierce civilization
of female introversion
come down from expectations,
from distant lofty rooms.

I have made days, children,
fed bodies and minutes with love,
spilled out milk from breasts and pitchers
over the mornings' insistent thresholds.
I have split myself open like a pomegranate
over my aborted and unborn children.
I have tried
to transform an encounter into permanence,
to encompass in man
his diversity.

But how what I encompassed
has now turned against me
and the created days fall apart
and the mornings over the pitchers
and the believed in minutes
and out of passion is born insult
enmity, sexual egoism
and on the attempted structure

the pitiless
blows of the mattock.

What great labor to create for oneself a body,
to awaken in it, in itself, a truth.
And now that I possess one, and the man
at woman's height is moulded in me
in the welded curves of growth,

now the body is mature grows old dies.

PER RIENTRARE IN ME, PER ACCETTARE

Per rientrare in me, per accettare
voci di saggi greci e di chi giunse
da Ippona fra le nebbie del Naviglio,
tante strade ho cercato: e mi guidavano
ora in fortezze ambigue, in borghi spenti,
ora in ossessionanti labirinti,
ora, era peggio, in strade luminose
che ad una svolta s'aprono nel mito.
Pensavo mi aiutassero le albe
boreali del Nord, le solitudini
dei bar dove le donne allineate
annegano la cenere degli anni
in whisky solitari, e si ritrova
all'odore la strada dell'albergo
o a un tocco di campane. Invece sono
qui, fra velieri chiari e scompigliate
zagare di scirocco, sola e non sola,
finalmente, qui intatta fra i miei numi
segreti e insieme fra volti di amici,
e il dialogo m'è nato, e più nessuno,
forse, saccheggia al buio il grano d'oro
che prima in sotterranei nasceva,
più bianco di quel grano dei sepolcri.

PREGHIERA PAGANA

Salva la foglia rossa di quest'inverno ardente,
distíllane il liquore memorabile,
tàtuami sul corpo quel reticolo di vene,
nelle conchiglie del capo incidimi il rombo del mare.

Il mondo sappia che lo abbiamo addentato
come un bel frutto colto nel suo destino ascendente,
che abbiamo bevuto alle fonti per farne un sangue vivo,
che nessun Ercole osava più alzarci colonne.

MARIA LUISA SPAZIANI (1924–)

TO RETREAT INTO MYSELF, TO ACCEPT

To retreat into myself, to accept
the voices of Greek sages and of him who
came from Hippo* through the mists of the Naviglio**
I have sought many ways: and they would lead me
now to dubious fortresses, to dead towns,
now into worrying labyrinths,
now, and it was worse, into shining streets
that at a turning opened into myth.
I thought that the boreal dawns of the North
would help me, the solitudes
of bars where rows of women
drown the ash of years
in solitary whiskies, and the way back
to the inn is found by the smell
or by a bell's chime. Instead I am
here, among the bright sailboats and ruffled
orange blossoms of the sirocco, alone and not alone,
at last, here intact among my secret
gods and among friendly faces at the same time,
and the dialogue has come to life in me, and no one
any longer, perhaps, pillages in the dark the golden grain
that earlier was born underground,
whiter than the grain from sepulchres.

*St. Augustine "came from Hippo."
**The Naviglio is a canal in Milan.

PAGAN PRAYER

Preserve the red leaf of this burning winter,
distill its memorable liquor,
tattoo on my body this network of veins,
in the shells of my head engrave the roar of the sea.

Let the world know that we have bitten into it
like a fine fruit gathered at the peak of its destiny,
that we have drunk at its springs and made living blood from them,
that no Hercules longer dared to raise pillars there.

E quando l'infame mammut ci avrà sgretolato le ossa,
e l'anima e la casa dei più lontani nipoti,
fai che attraverso l'ambra, come le felci dell'Etna,
il sole avvolga ancora la nostra filigrana.

REQUIEM PER SYLVIA PLATH

Un requiem per te
ogni volta che mi chino
a staccare lo spaghetto appiccicato
sul verde campo di battaglia
del grès della cucina, dal nitido
lancinante dolore
a una foglia di prezzemolo.

Un requiem per te mentre mi batto
con l'angustia del recinto
delle forze, povere stanghe di legno,
rinchiuso nell'altro più grande
dell'essere, alla soglia
del bosco umido del sonno
dove qualche cosa ci lava.

La via d'uscita è là? Nel buio
per te, almeno. Inginocchiata
stacco con l'unghia una piccola crosta
mentre dico un requiem per te.

And when the infamous mammoth has broken up our bones,
and the spirit and home of our most distant grandchildren,
force, through the amber, like the ferns of Etna,
the sun still to shine around our filigree.

LUCIANA FREZZA   (1926–)

REQUIEM FOR SYLVIA PLATH

A requiem for you
each time I lean over
to detach a bit of spaghetti caught
on the green battlefield
of the kitchen stoneware, from the bright
shooting pain
to a sprig of parsley.

A requiem for you while I struggle
against the narrowness of the enclosure
of my forces, poor wooden staves,
enclosed in the other greater one
of being, on the threshold
of the damp shrubbery of sleep
where something cleanses us.

Is the way out there? In the darkness
for you, at least. Kneeling
I detach with my nail a tiny crust
while I say a requiem for you.

NON POTRÒ PIÙ RIDERE DI VERA ALLEGRIA

Non potrò più ridere di vera allegria
non potrò mai avere parole che servano
dubiterò pure di quelle
che credevo colme di vero calore
potrò solo verificare l'errore quotidiano
le mostruose complicazioni la malattia incurabile
i parti deformi gli omicidi la guerra
le infezioni dell'aria radioattiva.
Gli uomini sono irragionevoli deboli e vili.
Io ho rinunciato a mettere al mondo un figlio.

LA SCALA A CHIOCCIOLA

Chiuse le imposte
smorzate tutte le lampade
serrati i polsi dietro la schiena
passo dopo passo
continuiamo a discendere
nel buio fitto dei luoghi comuni
la scala a chiocciola interminabile
dell'eversione quotidiana
tendendo le orecchie sgomenti
al rumore dei passi
sinistramente sonanti
delle prevaricazioni
i centogambe ferrati del potere
che sistematicamente ci seguono.
Tanto fitta la nebbia
che ci può capitare
di spacciare per storia
l'oroscopo del giorno
proclamando con feroce ironia
l'anno della donna nel nome di Maria.

ANNA MALFAIERA (1926–)

I CAN NO LONGER LAUGH WITH REAL JOY

I can no longer laugh with real joy
I can no longer use words with any meaning
I even doubt the ones
I had thought were full of real warmth
I can only confirm the daily error
the monstrous complications the incurable disease
the deformed limbs the murders the war
the contagions from the radioactive air.
Men are irrational weak and vile.
Into this world I refuse to bring a child.

LIANA CATRI (1929–)

THE SPIRAL STAIRCASE

Shutters closed
all lights put out
wrists tied behind our backs
step after step
we continue to go down
in the pitch darkness of common places
the interminable spiral staircase
of daily destruction
straining our fearful ears
for the sound of footsteps
ominously resonating
of breaches of trust
the iron-shod centipedes of power
that systematically follow us.
So dense is the fog
that it can happen to us
to pass off the day's horoscope
as history
proclaiming with ferocious irony
the year of the woman in the name of Mary.

Celebrare coi violini l'impostura
con tutto il rispetto del maschile
fa parte del programma
in questo sacrale paese
di supermaschi nostrani
ufficialetti blasonati
scoperti nell'araldica
della pubblicità stradale
in questo fallico bosco di miti
in servizio permanente effettivo
dove è albero l'uomo
femminile l'ombra
che nasce ai suoi piedi
(per troppi vivere di riflesso è norma)
penisola privata di silenzio
con riserva di caccia
azzurra
con la solita meccanica dei gesti
solo nei versi dei poeti.
In tanto lucido nero
scivola l'angoscia.
Quante le donne scultura
in bella mostra su ogni scalino
a coniugare in coro
il passivo dei verbi?

LO SDRUCCIOLO CUORE CHE IN ME È RIBELLE

Lo sdrucciolo cuore che in me è ribelle
quasi sempre in me preferirebbe
una più saggia angoscia
l'animo è davvero poca cosa
è davvero
infernale così come tu dici.

Ma credevo nel soldo e nella miseria
assieme assetati di vendetta: o credevo
nel lento pellegrinaggio ad una fonte

Celebrating the imposture with violins
with all the respect of the male
is part of the program
in this blessed country
of homegrown supermales
emblazoned subalterns
revealed in the heraldry
of roadside publicity
in this phallic forest of myths
in permanent effective service
where man is tree
female the shade
born at his feet
(for too many men living by reflex is normal)
private peninsula of silence
with blue
hunting reserve
with the usual mechanics of gestures
only in the verses of poets.
In so much shining black
anguish slips in.
How many women does sculpture
beautifully show on every stair
conjugating in chorus
the passive of verbs?

AMELIA ROSSELLI (1930-)

THE DACTYLIC HEART THAT IN ME IS A REBEL

The dactylic heart that in me is a rebel
would almost always rather have in me
a wiser anguish
the mind is really so unimportant
it's really
hellish the way that you say.

But I believed in wages and poverty
thirsting together for revenge: or I believed
in the slow pilgrimage to a source

dedicata ad un pubblico e anche privatissimo
dibattito, che essa ingigantisce
così ingegnosa.

Nessuna fede ha mai mosso le montagne
tu muovi le montagne in me, tu che sei
compagno di un momento e senza amore
con quel tuo chiarore di corta vita
l'estate stessa spiovente
nel suo abracadabra di giovinezza irresponsabile
ricevo dalle tue abbondanti e magrissime
braccia.

MIO ANGELO, IO NON SEPPI MAI QUALE ANGELO

Mio angelo, io non seppi mai quale angelo
fosti, o per quali vie storte ti amai
o venerai, tu che scendendo ogni gradino
sembravi salirli, frustarmi, mostrarmi
una via tutta perduta alla ragione, quando
facesti al caso quel che esso riprometteva,
cioè mi lasciasti.

Non seppi nemmeno perché tra tanti chiarori
eccitati dell'intelletto in pena, vi
furono così sotterranee evcluzioni d'un
accordarsi al mio, al vostro e tuo bisogno
d'una sterilità completa.

Eppure eccomi qua, a scrivere versi,
come se fosse non del tutto astratto
alla mia ricerca d'un enciclopedico
capire quasi tutto a me offerto senza
lo spazio d'una volontà di ferro a controllare
quel poco del tutto così mal offerto.

dedicated to a public and also very private
debate, which the so ingenious source
would magnify.

No belief has ever moved mountains
you move mountains in me, you who are
the companion of a moment and without love
with that shortlived brilliance of yours
summer itself flowing away
in its abracadabra of irresponsible youth
I receive from your abundant and thinnest
arms.

MY ANGEL, I NEVER KNEW WHAT ANGEL

My angel, I never knew what angel
you were, or through what twisted ways I loved you
or worshipped you, who coming down each stair
seemed to be going up them, to punish me, to show me
a way wholly lost to reason, when
you took the opportunity to do the expected,
that is you left me.

I didn't even know why among so many excited
flashes of intellect in pain, there
were such underground evolutions of an
agreement with mine, with your friends and your need
for a complete sterility.

However, here I am, writing verses,
as if it were not wholly separate
from my encyclopedic research
to understand almost the whole offered me without
room for an iron will to control
that small piece of the whole so badly offered.

The poem, "On Fatherish Men," was written in English.

ON FATHERISH MEN

  Great Pompous Ague, and Vapid Arguments
do they use, to Use you. The Branch is Loaded
with Ripe Oats, smothered into the Air. With Tinkling fingers
I do Shake it down. So you would have me 'pon your Knees
quite Freely? Pay then First! Then will I Join you
at the Feverish tree, and sing a song of
Exstasie (short-cut, 'tis the Youths we Turn to).
Or would Ye be my Grande-Father? No, too Dulle this proves:
an Olde Man, well ripe in Lust,
or None. Thine Fine Rumbuctious Talk
but Whiffs at Me; 'tis the Bed I want, and
Respect of my Maidenhood, too: till you Die
of Excess. Would you Return (after Judiciously
Leaving me) and take up Habits again? Then come Crawling
'pon your two blind Knees. Have thee not recognized I bee
a Devilish Maiden, pulling at Thy flucid Beard? Yet
I do Love thee, and beg thee be
a True Father. Mine is Gone
into the Grave, waving a Banner
of Idiocee: be thou more Intelligent; Keep
from Policee, and Take Mee. Humbly shall I
Spit at thee, Crawling my Hand at your Hind-
Pocket, as you Kisse Me. But no Lucrous
Intents had I, see; twas but to wipe the Loaden sea
of my Love-tears, with Thine Hankerchiee. Come, come,
be though Brave, and Come to Mee,
a-Loaden with rich Jewelree. All Night long
shall we Curry the Milke 'f Innocenciee.

NOTTURNO

Angells affect us oft, and worship'd bee
                    John Donne

Oggi ora in questo momento il mondo mi vola addosso.
Non ho fatto, nei giorni passati,
che guardare paesaggi
lagune isole moriture colline tronfie ancora per poco
lunghe soporose arcate accudite da gechi e lumache:
morti arcaici animali premurosi di morte cose. Questo,
tutto questo
si vede quando già
il proprio sangue naviga lontano, doppia
nella tempesta il capo Horn
quando il rossore della carne
avvilisce nella grotta del vampiro, e il seme
della continuazione
appartiene a provette grafiche
sospese in un laboratorio sotterraneo.

Le carte sparse in questo tavolo, come somigliano
alle suppellettili della morte:
questo foglio è una tibia sguarnita
e questo quaderno una lampada dove l'olio finí in fretta
in una chiarata convulsa e sbilenca;
le altre robe scritte sono abiti che il defunto
non può piú indossare
e vanno per il robivecchi.

L'abito che vedete qui, usatelo per vestire il cadavere
aggiustategli sopra una ciocca di fiori che tolga
lo stantio di questi vecchi materiali da costruzione.
Vi sorrido e vi saluto col fazzoletto
affaciata da una casa lontana.

ROSSANA OMBRES (1931–)

NOCTURNE

Angells affect us oft, and worship'd bee
                    John Donne

Today now at this moment the world flies against me.
I have done nothing in the past days
but look at landscapes
lagoons doomed islands hills puffed up for a while longer
wide drowsy arches cared for by lizards and snails;
dead archaic animals solicitous of dead things. This,
all this
is seen when already
our own blood is sailing far away, doubling
Cape Horn in the storm
when the redness of flesh
degenerates in the vampire's cave, and the seed
of continuity
is the property of graphic test tubes
hung in a subterranean laboratory.

The papers scattered on this table, how like they are
to the trappings of death:
this sheet is a tibia stripped bare
and this notebook a lamp where the oil ran out quickly
in a convulsed and twisted egg-white poultice;
the other written things are clothes that the deceased
can no longer wear
and are ready for the thrift shop.

The cloak you see here, use it to clothe the corpse
over it arrange a bunch of flowers to take away
the staleness of these old building materials.
I am smiling at you and wave my handkerchief to you
as I watch from a distant house.

MADRE SORELLA

Madre cos'è successo in principio
nel buio di te
quando ho voluto così ferocemente esistere
nella placenta dove ho affondato
le mie radici di libertà
l'urlo di esplosa follia
che mi ha scagliato alla luce
—lacerazione fuga
credi che non lo sappia—
sanguinando allo strappo
delle nostre incastrate infelicità
così totalmente distruggendo di noi
ogni diversa possibilità
la brutta copia di me
la sorella nera che avrei potuto essere
per questa soluzione definitiva
una donna
madre sorella me stessa
potenzialmente la più bianca
e immortale creatura della specie
interamente nascosta dal corpo
sottoposta a questa terribile biologia
buco nero che ha atterrito la storia
lupa affamata
feroce con se stessa
muta da sempre
una che impara da principio
a contare le assenze
la treccia penzolante nel vuoto
fare l'appello di abbandoni e recuperi
misurare lo spazio
dall'esserci o non esserci di un volto
giocare la vita su presagi e ricordi
ciò che non fu mai vero o forse lo era
ma di che fragile e breve verità
—sarà mai stato madre per noi due?—

Ma cosa sarà
di questi figli del mito
nati nei labirinti della fuga
mantenuti nel possibile

FRANCA MARIA CATRI (1931–)

SISTER MOTHER

Mother what happened in the beginning
in your darkness
when I wanted so fiercely to exist
in the placenta where I sank down
my roots of freedom
the howl of explosive madness
that flung me into the light
—laceration escape
you think I don't know—
bleeding at the tearing
of our embedded unhappiness
thus totally destroying for us
all possibility of difference
the rough copy of me
the black sister that I could have been
through this definitive solution
a woman
mother sister myself
potentially the whitest
and most immortal creature of the species
wholly hidden by the body
subjected to this terrible biology
black hole that has terrified history
starving she-wolf
fierce with herself
eternally silent
someone who learns from the beginning
to reckon the absences
the braid hanging in the void
to call the roll of abandonments and rescues
to measure the space
between the presence and the absence of a face
to gamble life on presentiments and memories
that which never was true or perhaps was
only of such fragile and brief truth
—will it ever have been mother for us two?—

But what will become
of the mythical children
born in the labyrinths of escape
maintained in the possible

da un latte di ghiaccio
padri amanti fratelli
cervi spauriti
dal sesso dolce di pesca
faraoni impotenti
che il potere ha perduto
teneri adolescenti degli stupri
figli voraci dal cuore di mandorla
nostra colpa segreta.

Immagina un crollo
chiaro e gioioso
i muri aperti a una finestra totale
i nostri occhi primi occhi del mondo
mani incantate
al sesso duro dei frutti.
Non moriremo più.

Va bene madre
partoriscimi pure.
Voglio con tanta forza la vita
che potrei morire nel desiderio.
Per tutti gli anni
che il nostro sangue ha nutrito
dal segreto dei cessi
la placenta della terra
voglio così forte la nostra libertà
in questo rosso girotondo di sfida
voglio così forte cantare
che il canto potrebbe rompermi il cuore
e continuare a vivere
senza di me.

by an icy milk
fathers lovers brothers
bucks terrified
by peach-sweet sex
impotent pharoahs
whom power has ruined
rapes' tender adolescents
ravenous children with almond hearts
our secret crime.

Imagine a fall
clear and joyous
walls open to a total window
our eyes the first eyes of the world
hands fascinated
at the hard sex of fruit.
We shall die no more.

All right mother
give birth to me please.
I wish for life with such strength
that I could die in the desire.
Because of all the years
that our blood has nourished
with the privacy of latrines
the earth's placenta
I want so strongly our freedom
in the red round dance of defiance
I want to sing so strongly
that the song could break my heart
and go on living
without me.

LA GRANDE PAURA

La storia della mia persona
è la storia di una grande paura
di essere me stessa,
contrapposta alla paura di perdere me stessa,
contrapposta alla paura della paura.

Non poteva essere diversamente:
nell'apprensione si perde la memoria,
nella sottomissione tutto.

Non poteva
la mia infanzia,
saccheggiata dalla famiglia,
consentirmi una maturità stabile, concreta.
Né la mia vita isolata
consentirmi qualcosa di meno fragile
di questo dibattermi tra ansie e incertezze.

All'infanzia sono sopravvissuta,
all'età adulta sono sopravvissuta.
Quasi niente rispetto alla vita.
Sono sopravvissuta, però,
E adesso, tra le rovine del mio essere,
qualcosa, una ferma utopia, sta per fiorire.

PIANISSIMO

sí
vienimi in
          contro
pregando sempre
prega lei
respirando meglio
adesso
sussurra
affettuosamente

e poi?
la scena si ripete

PIERA OPPEZZO (1934–)

THE GREAT FEAR

The history of my self
is the history of a great fear
of being myself,
set against the fear of losing myself,
set against the fear of fear.

It could not be otherwise:
in apprehension memory is lost,
in submission everything.

Nor could
my childhood,
ransacked by my family,
permit me a stable, definite maturity.
Nor could my isolated life
permit me a less fragile thing
than this floundering among anxieties and uncertainties.

My childhood I survived,
my adulthood I survived.
Almost nothing compared with life.
I survived, nevertheless.
And now, among the ruins of my being,
something, a firm utopia, is about to flower.

VERY SOFTLY

yes
come and meet
           me
always asking
she asks
breathing better
now
whispers
affectionately

and then?
the scene is repeated

(in questo è il
                    senso)
ma poi è poco
così fragile
non si ha idea
così un po' sudata
così un po' di febbre
un po' di euforia
tensione soprattutto
                              un po'
minacciosa
paziente leggermente
sfiora e dice
ooohhh
con un bel tono in
                        certo

GN IS HAPPY

(a Isabella)

Lui nuota e io nuoto e non nuotano solo i laghi nei
capelli (la barca la ringhiera la riva del disegno
giapponese nelle punte).
Scendendo.
Scendendo gli anemoni di mare pulsano aria
le bocche di tanti pesci
da squalo che fende da pesce rosso quasi immobile da
trota da tinca da carpa e poi

CAPRA E CAPRONE!

Il serpente sotto il piede la mano serpente che sale
su per le gambe la lunga lingua sottile e biforcuta
che esce dalla bocca

MARIA E POI BISCIA AL SOLE

Smettila Tom Jones! Stop it please stop it
Tom Jones!
Ma lui dice cavallo e io lo cavalco e m'inarco

(in this is the
                    meaning)
but then it's tiny
so fragile
one has no idea
so a little sweaty
so a little feverish
a little euphoria
above all tension
                    a little
threatening
patient lightly
caresses and says
ooohhh
with a fine tone un
                    certain

GIULIA NICCOLAI   (1934–)

GN IS HAPPY

(to Isabella)

He swims and I swim and not only the lakes in our
hair swim (the boat the railing the Japanese-drawing
shore in the ends).
Descending.
Descending the sea anemones pulsate air
the mouths of many fish
from cleaving shark from almost motionless goldfish from
trout from tench from carp and then

SHE-GOAT AND HE-GOAT!

The serpent underfoot the serpent hand that rises
along the legs the long thin forked tongue
that darts from the mouth

MARIA AND THEN WATER-SNAKE IN THE SUN

Stop it Tom Jones! Stop it please stop it
Tom Jones!
But he says horse and I ride him and arch my back

(ALICE SULLE GINOCCHIA DI DODGSON)

e vestita siedo come un cosacco sfinito.
Lui dice cavallo e mi cavalca
shameless brazen hussy girati
adesso ti devo mordere la schiena.

LA CAVALLA DIVENTA LA SCIMMIA

e la schiena diventa la bocca che morde la schiena

SONO ANCHE UNA CAMMELLA. Non vuoi?

Mi sai muovere mi sai commuovere (non avevo mai
capito prima d'ora che Otello e Desdemona sono
la stessa persona). In inglese

YOU KNOW HOW TO MOVE ME

significa entrambe le cose fiato di ghibli
e canna d'organo.
Viviamo di notte e facciamo l'alba
facciamo questo bel lavoretto ben fatto
che è il fare l'alba.
Alba fatta capo ha

E DI GIORNO SI FA IL RESTO DEL CORPO.

Ognuno vuol dare una forma ai propri desideri.

(Continua)

Se tu al fiume ci porti Elle Elle
io ci porto Isabella!

(ALICE ON DODGSON'S KNEES)

and when dressed I sit like a Cossack in a faint.
He says horse and he rides me
shameless brazen hussy turn around
now I have to bite your back.

THE MARE BECOMES THE MONKEY

and the back becomes the mouth that bites the back

I AM ALSO A CAMEL. Wouldn't you like that?

You know how to make me move you know how to move me (until
     now
I never understood that Othello and Desdemona were
the same person). In English

YOU KNOW HOW TO MOVE ME

means both things dry-wind breath
and organ reed.
We live at night and make the dawn
we do this lovely well-wrought work
which is the making of the dawn.
What's done is dawn

AND DURING THE DAY WE MAKE THE REST OF OUR BODIES.

Each of us wants to give a shape to our own desires.

                                        (*To be continued*)

If you take us to the river Elle Elle
I'll bring Isabella!

—*Beverly Allen*

DALL'ESTERNO IL MOTIVO ADEGUATO

Dall'esterno il motivo adeguato,
l'apparenza subito necessaria.
Di volta in volta gli oggetti e gli eventi
la necessità indispensabile, la partecipazione
delle convergenze.
Lontano dall'impulso iniziale, dalla continua
sedimentazione.
Sfuggendo a modifiche, apporti, soppressioni.
Allora sembra chiaro.
E per l'appunto,
lí ci si specchia.

AI MIEI FIGLI

Tu farai egli farà voi farete
tu sarai egli sarà voi sarete.
Basta, come posso insegnarvi
il futuro, accidenti, in questo
limbo fottuto di presente?
Convincetevene, come vi posso
dire: questo sì, l'altro no?
Senza radici,
un chilometro più indietro
non sono qua
non vi posso dire
quel che si fa e quel che faremo.
Tu poi, è tempo
che pensi a cosa farai fra cinque o sei anni;
ti rivolgi a me
che diavolo vuoi che ti dica
che sarei orgogliosa di un buon ingegnere
o di vederti trapiantare cervelli?
Vi deprimo, vi frustro, lo so:
laceratemi me lo merito.

FROM OUTSIDE COMES THE ADEQUATE CAUSE

From outside comes the adequate cause,
the suddenly necessary appearance.
Now and then the objects and the events
the indispensable necessity, the participation
of convergences.
Far from the initial impulse, from the continuous
sedimentation.
Fleeing modifications, contributions, suppressions.
Then it seems clear.
And, in fact,
there we mirror ourselves.

—*Beverly Allen*

ROSANNA GUERRINI   (1935–)

TO MY CHILDREN

You will do he will do you will do
You will be he will be you will be.
That's enough, how can I teach you
the future, dammit, in this
fucked-up limbo of the present?
Get this into your heads, how can I
tell you this, yes, the other, no?
Without roots,
a kilometer further behind
I am not here
I cannot tell you
what one does and what we shall do.
You, then, it is time
you were thinking of what you will do in five or six years;
you turn to me
what the devil do you want me to tell you
that I should be proud of a good engineer
or to see you transplanting brains?
I depress you, I frustrate you, I know:
tear me apart I deserve it.

Mi fanno ridere quelli
che a tavola
parlano coi figli
della Cecoslovacchia
della Cina
di Rudi il Rosso,
tronfi tacchini,
lo farei anch'io,
ma le labbra cucite
mi si muove solo il braccio
per un manrovescio
se vi si intinge
la manica nel piatto.
Andiamo in campagna
spunta l'erba, un formicaio
un buco di talpa
ma un dubbio un sospetto
nell'aria
di coatto.
La vostra gioia non avrà durata
perché partorita
da madre senza radice,
la mia linfa secca si
nutrirebbe di un pasto
di foglie verdi
che madre mi rifiuta,
mi lacererete figli, un giorno, io che
vi insegno la non vita?

LE POESIE DELLE DONNE

''Le poesie delle donne sono spesso
piatte, ingenue, realistiche e ossessive''
mi dice un critico gentile dagli occhi a palla.
''Mancano di leggerezza, di fumo, di vanità,
sono tutte d'un pezzo come dei tubi,
non c'è garbo, scioltezza, estro;

Those people make me laugh
who talk
with their children at meals
about Czechoslovakia
about China
about Rudi the Red,*
pompous turkeys,
I'd do that too,
but my lips are sewn shut
only my arm moves
for a backhanded slap
if you dip
your sleeve in the dish.
Let's go to the country
the grass is sprouting, an anthill
a mole hole
but in the air
a doubt a suspicion
of being forced.
Your joy will not last
because it is birthed
from a rootless mother,
my dried-up juices
might be nourished by a meal
of green leaves
that mother refuses me,
will you tear me apart one day, children, I who
teaches you non-life?

*Rudi the Red, a German Marxist, led students' revolts in the spring of 1968.

DACIA MARAINI (1936–)

POEMS BY WOMEN

"Poems by women are frequently
flat, naive, realistic and obsessive,"
a kindly round-eyed critic tells me.
"They lack lightness, vapor, frivolity,
they are all of a piece like tubes,
they have no grace, fluency, or inspiration;

sono prive dell'intelligenza maliziosa
dell'artificio, insomma non raggiungono
quell'aria da pomeriggio limpido dopo la pioggia.''

Forse è vero, gli dico. Ma tu non sai
cosa vuol dire essere donna. Dovresti
provare una volta per piacere anche se
è proibito dal tuo sesso di pane e ferro.
Ride. Strabuzza gli occhi. ''A me non importa
se sia donna o meno. Voglio vedere i risultati
poetici. C'è chi riesce a fare la ciambella
con il buco. Se è donna o uomo cosa cambia?''

Cambia, amico dagli occhi verdi, cambia;
perché una donna non può fare finta
di non essere donna. Ed essere donna
significa conoscere la propria soggezione,
significa vivere e respirare la degradazione
e il disprezzo di sé che si può superare
solo con fatiche dolorose e lagrime nere.

È per questo che tante si rifugiano
nella passività, nell'ordine costituito,
perché hanno paura di quella fatica e
di quelle lagrime che sono necessarie per
riscattare la propria umanità perduta
come un dente di latte, chissà quando,
nel processo sibillino della crescita sociale.

Una mattina un padre generosa ha
legato il tuo dente al pomello della porta
che poi ha spalancato con un calcio e
addio dente di miele che ti faceva bambina
e ancora inconsapevole del ruolo pacato
e gelido che ti aspetta ora come un
cappotto fiorato appeso nell'ingresso e
se vai fuori devi indossarlo se no
rishci di morire assiderata e pesta.

Una donna che scrive poesie e sa di
essere donna, non può che tenersi attaccata
stretta ai contenuti perché la sofisticazione
delle forme è una cosa che riguarda il potere
e il potere che ha la donnà è sempre un
non-potere, una eredità scottante e mai del tutto sua.

La sua voce sarà forse dura e terragna
ma è la voce di una leonessa che è stata

they are devoid of the mischievous wit
of artifice, in short they don't achieve
that air of a shining afternoon after rain."

It may be true, I reply. But you don't know
what being a woman means. You ought to
try it sometime, please, even if
it's forbidden by your bread-and-iron sex.
He laughs. He rolls his eyes. "I don't care
whether or not I'm a woman. I want to see the poetic
results. There are those who can make donuts
with holes: Does it matter whether they're men or women?"

It matters, my green-eyed friend, it matters;
because a woman is unable to pretend
that she's not a woman. And to be a woman
means to know her own state of subjection,
it means to live and breathe the humiliation
and self-contempt that can be overcome
only by painful toil with black tears.

This is why so many women hide
within passivity, in the established order,
because they're afraid of that toil
and those tears that are necessary to
redeem their own humanity lost
like a milk tooth, heaven knows when,
in the sibylline process of social growth.

One morning a well-meaning father
tied your tooth to the handle of the door
then slammed it shut with a kick and
farewell honeyed tooth that marked you a child
and still unconscious of the frigid
and tranquillized role that now awaits you like a
flowered cloak hanging in the hall and
which if you go out you must put on or else
risk dying frost-bitten and crushed.

A woman who writes poetry and knows that
she is a woman can only make herself stick
closely to the subject because sophistication
of form is something that goes with power
and the power a woman has is always a
non-power, a burning inheritance never wholly hers.

Her voice will perhaps be harsh and earthen
but it's the voice of a lioness who has been

tenuta pecora per troppo tempo assennato.
È una voce fiacca, grezza e mutilata
che viene da lontano, da fuori della
storia, dall'inferno degli sfruttati.
Un inferno che non migliora la gente
come si crede, ma la rende pigra,
malata e nemica di se stessa.

MADRE CANINA

Dita canine, madre, moglie, bue,
della tua delinquenza mi sono disperata,
della tua allegria feroce e dei tuoi
lampanti capricci, mi sono domandata,
mi sono diagnosticata, la tua purezza
senza storia, la tua dolce inesistenza,
madre canina, moglie, sorella, i tuoi canti
sfiatati, le tue dolcezze serali, io ricordo
tutto, anche l'odore del tuo mestruo e il
sapore delle guance affaticate, e lo zampettio
dei tuoi stivali e lo spostamento orizzontale
dei tuoi fianchi d'un bianco sconcertante,
madre, figlia, generatrice, una filaccia di
morte e una furia nervosa ti incorona il petto,
non voglio dirti che mi sei nemica, la tua
colpevolezza è dei quattro venti e si nutre
di azoto, dal rosso delle tue unghie mattutine,
dal castagno dei tuoi capelli di laniccio, dalla
tua gola consenziente, dai tuoi denti di furbizia,
dalle tue larghe mammelle di amichevoli cavalle,
mi viene giù un rivolo di pena e non vorrei
chiamarti nemica, da quando hai perso la
coscienza, da quando l'hai resa calcarea e
scintillante come la perla dei tuoi bronchi,
da quando la tua inerzia ti ha rammollito i
fianchi, da quando in un prato disteso e secco
della tua ariosa testa non giochi più e neghi e
neghi paurosamente chinandoti sull'orifizio
della mortalità e della delusione dei sensi.

taken for a sheep for too much prudent time.
It is a feeble voice, crude and mutilated
that comes from a long way off, from beyond
history, from the hell of the exploited.
A hell which does not improve people
as is believed, but makes them lazy,
sick, and enemies of themselves.

CANINE MOTHER

Canine fingers, mother, wife, ox,
your delinquency has driven me to despair,
your fierce cheerfulness and your
brilliant vagaries I have wondered about,
made up diagnoses for, and your purity
without fuss, your gentle nonexistence,
canine mother, wife, sister, your breathless
songs, your evening sweetness, I remember
it all, even your menstrual smell and the
flavor of your tired cheeks, and the pattering
of your boots and the horizontal shifting
of your disconcertingly white flanks,
mother, daughter, creatrix, a raveling of
death and a nervous rage crowns your breast,
I don't want to tell you that you are my enemy, your
guilt belongs to the four winds and feeds on
nitrogen, from the red of your morning nails,
from the chestnut of your fleecy hair, from
your consenting throat, from your cunning teeth,
from your big friendly mares' breasts,
a stream of pain flows down on me and I don't want
to call you enemy, since you have lost
consciousness, since you have made it calcareous and
shining like the pearl of your bronchia,
since your inertia has softened your
flanks, since in a wide and dry meadow
of your airy head you no longer play, and you deny and
deny fearfully leaning over the orifice
of mortality and of the delusion of the senses.

PERCHÈ NON HO VOLUTO CHIEDERE

amore che macini
sempre gli stessi ceci
senza assaggiare mai la farinata
o il pane e panelle

da o bleu si precipita
a oblò senza luce
per orti fragolosi si arranca a inciampo
di ortiche vetrose

dentro il nucleo non c'è punto fermo

o quest'amore che brucia
zolfanello per cucina
povera

perché non ho voluto chiedere
l'avevo immaginato

un ritmo di maderna
per il tuo flauto di gazzelloni
—piccola tachicardia
nella subordinata del rifiuto

il mio amore non ha casa
l'hanno sfrattato
e non sa piú dove sta

JOLANDA INSANA (1937–)

BECAUSE I DID NOT WANT TO ASK

love, you're always
grinding the same grain
never tasting the porridge
or the bread and pastry

from oh bleu we fall
to a lightless porthole
through strawberried gardens we hobble and stumble
over vitreous nettles

inside the nucleus there is no firm point

oh this love which burns
a wooden match for barren
kitchens

because I did not want to ask
I had imagined

a maderna rhythm
for your gazzelloni flute
—little tachycardia
in the subordinate clause of refusal

my love has no home
they evicted it
it no longer knows where it lives

—Keala Jane Jewell

RACCORDO ANULARE

Non dimenticheremo nulla.
Non gli uomini che dalle idee sono stati scelti.
Né i loro massacri.
Né i loro miti.
Non dimenticheremo che avete avuto un sesso.
Un sesso alla memoria!
Senza giungere mai ad essere persone.
Non dimenticheremo i privilegi, la rispettabilità
gli onori
che vi siete guadagnati senza mai essere uomini.
Benedetti
benedetti
benedetti
i vostri bambini quando
improvvisamente
capiranno.

Al governo il partito usuraio!
Al Monte di Pietà i voti proletari.

Non dimenticheremo la linea costruttiva ed usueta
del tradimento collettivo.
Non dimenticheremo la foia di *voler essere*.
La foia di avere.
La foia degli amori possessivi
e l'odio che voi chiamate ambizione.
La foia della periferia che mira...
E mira giusto, no?
Alla cattedrale del potere.

Noi non dimenticheremo le tue donne, benpensante.
Donne sante e tremende
frutto del ventre tuo cerebrale-borghese.
Democratico!
Le tue donne: che da sempre si sono tirate su le maniche
per l'opinabile consenso di tirarsi giù le brache.
Donne che annaffiano quotidiane
il fiore del mirtillo in segreto allevando
uomini-marmellata.

'Essere donne'...
Dalla cameriera alla sera

SANDRA MANGINI   (c. 1940–)

RING ROAD

We shall not forget anything.
Not the men who have been chosen by ideas.
Nor their massacres.
Nor their myths.
We shall not forget that you have had a sex.
A sex for memory!
Without ever managing to be people.
We shall not forget the privileges, the respectability
the honors
that you have won for yourselves without ever being men.
Blessed be
blessed be
blessed be
your children when
suddenly
they understand.

Let's elect the moneylender party!
Send the proletarian votes to the Pawnshop.

We shall not forget the constructive and customary line
of a collective betrayal.
We shall not forget the lust of *wanting to be*.
The lust of having.
The lust of possessive loves
and the hatred you call ambition.
The lust of the outskirts that aims...
And aims right, doesn't it?
At the cathedral of power.

We shall not forget your women, you conservative,
Saintly women and tremendous
fruit of your cerebral-bourgeois belly.
Christian Democrat!
Your women: who have always rolled up their sleeves
for the conceivable permission to pull down their pants.
Daily women who water
the bilberry flower in secret raising
marmalade-men.

"To be women"...
From maid until evening

dal marito al mattino
nel pomeriggio il bambino.

Essere donne: più o meno per procura.
Essere donne con prestabilita misura.
Essere donne.
E perchenno?
No.

Inguini intellettuali.
Casalinghe.
Impiegate.
Operaie tailleur Chanell.
Tailleur Chanell.
Odorono.
Cattoliche.
Colgate.

Essere donne?
Autentiche mai.
Sperma molto.
Uomini mai.

Denaro, presto!
Come non mai.
Insistere ancora.
Esistere mai.
Essere uomini—Essere donne—Come farai?

Non dimenticheremo i buoni.
I Buoni del Tesoro.
Non dimenticheremo il vostro Dio.

Segnalate il sorpasso.
Suonate forte i claxon della stampa!
Superate a sinistra...
Ma rientrate subito in corsia.
Stop a 300 m.

Imponete
hawg
huey
uh-ib

distruggete tutto ciò che si muove
non può essere Dio.
Rientrate alla base dopo la missione orgogliosi
con Dio.

from husband until morning
in the afternoon the child.

To be women: more or less by proxy.
To be women of pre-set measurements.
To be women.
And whynot?
No.

Intellectual groins.
Housewives.
Employees.
Chanel-suited workers.
Chanel suit.
Deodorant.
Catholics.
Colgate.

Be women?
Never authentic.
A lot of sperm.
Never men.

Money quick!
As never before.
Again insist.
Never exist.
Be men—Be women—How will you do it?

We won't forget the coupons.
The Treasury Bills.
We won't forget your God.

Honk when passing.
Sound loudly the horns of the press!
Pass on the left. . .
But return immediately to your lane.
Stop at 300 meters.

Impose
hawg
huey
uh-ib

destroy all that moves
it cannot be God.
Return to base after the mission proud
with God.

Controllate lo specchietto retrovisore, ora.
Vedete Dio?

All'ONU il raccordo anulare:
Santo Domingo.
Hannoy.
Il Pentagono—La Casa Bianca.
Democrazia U.S.A

All'ONU il raccordo anulare
di questa pace violenta
di questa pace collage
di teste di moro
di teste di giallo
per teste di bianco invece:
After shave and Atkinson for men.

da *PATERNALE*

Con dedica paternale a un padre patriarcale

III.
ma poi che ne sapete dei diritti di genitali soffocati
...nt'anni nella galera di famiglia? dei gerani da non toccare
perché 'mestruata'? delle grandi cose da
grandi del sesso (paterno) fava perpetuamente infavata
(infavante) dei nostri corpi invece infagottati
nella castità
    bambina che già zitellavo (grassa)
ovarica febbricitante sino a ventitreanni nella Casa
del Padre nella quale non ci sono mansioni diverse
ma una sola (la Sua i Suoi sbadigli la Sua
stitichezza la Sua fame i Suoi *divertissements*
camuffati da sublimazioni libridiche i Suoi
cantari la Sua pronuba Arte la Sua missa
dominicalis)
    a mandrie noi dietro le Sue gambe
alta-lenanti di nipote-di-prete saturo fino a che
strizzarlo non esce acqua di chiesa di missa mortis
latino religio italiotasettecentesca.

Look in your rear view mirror, now
Do you see God?

At the U.N. the ring road:
Santo Domingo.
Hanoi.
The Pentagon—The White House.
Democracy U.S.A.

At the U.N. the ring road
of this violent peace
of this collage peace
of moors' heads
of yellow heads
of white heads instead:
After shave and Atkinson for men.

MARIELLA BETTARINI (1942–)

from *PATERNAL*

With paternal dedication to a patriarchal father

III.
but then what do you know about the rights of suffocated genitals
...ty years in the family prison? of geraniums not to be touched
because "you're menstruating"? of big grown up things
about sex (paternal) the prick perpetually pricked
(pricking) our bodies all wrapped up instead
in chastity
        a little girl who was already becoming an old maid (fat)
feverishly ovaric until twenty-three years old in my Father's
House where there are not many mansions
but only one (His mansion His yawns His
constipation His hunger His *divertissements*
camouflaged by bookerotic sublimations His
singing His matchmaking Art His missa
domenicalis)
        we a flock behind His teeter-
tottering priest's nephew's legs saturated until
out comes church water to sprinkle him water of a Latin
missa mortis religio eighteenthcenturyidiotalian.

IV.
e quando le dicesti "non ho più commercio
con quella donna" non ti pareva quello un atto grosso
contro la nostra classe di donne-bambini sottoposta da secoli
al tu' potere?
    propri' allora nacque
la mi' rivolta il mi' riscatto principiò allora
a realizzarsi contro te grosso Padre del nostro pane
nostri sonni nostri vestiti nostri corpi
e di' donne l'un contro l'altra armate in attesa
                                   [ché non la "passione"

a entrambe davi ma il tu' potere adfirmavi
e la pietosa bassezza loro di donne:
l'una sanza diritti (con lo tuo amore) l'altra
col diritto a fregiarsi di un tuo
anello (ma sanza più l'alto amore tuo).
                                    [così
facesti me vendicativa (mistica sudaticcia grassa)
zitellante a vent'anni anorresica disappetente di tutto
mentre gustavi tu i doppi della tua "passioncella"
offendevi la persona magr'impotente che si formava:
il mi' occhio (sociale) guasto
    che di poi deviava (strabico)
sotto le note

COME IL BOTANICO

Sbalzata di classe in classe, rasento i muri
per la vergogna che la primavera incontri
il mio viso fluido e grigio ma,
per contro, esulto per la gioia
di condividere la sorte
di chi per strada va ad occhi bassi.

Anche ora—che il diciassette di aprile
sta per andare nel mucchio, e che la mia situazione
si direbbe di debolezza—
sento che le articolazioni malate
e il manto della tigre su un corpo di pecora
preludono a una libertà più grande,
magari quella della verità strappata a morsi,
anche perché a una donna non dicono mai
la verità intera, e se ella stessa la dice
la escludono dai lavori,

IV.

and when you told her "I no longer have anything to do
with that woman" didn't that seem a gross act
against our class of women-children subject for centuries
to your power?
        just then my
rebellion was born my redemption began then
to take shape against you fat Father of our bread
our sleep our clothes our bodies
and of women armed against each other waiting
        because it was not/"passion"
you were giving to both but you were asserting your power
and their pitiful women's lowliness:
one without rights (with your love) the other
with the right to deck herself out with a
ring of yours (but no longer with your deep love)
                                            this way
you made me vindictive (mystical sweaty fat)
oldmaidish at twenty anorexic no appetite for anything
while you were enjoying the duplicates of your "little passion"
you were offending the thin powerless person that was forming:
my damaged (social) eye
                that deviated (cross-eyed) from then on
under the notes

AS THE BOTANIST

Bounced from class to class, I hug the walls
for shame lest spring encounter
my grey and fluid face, yet,
on the other hand, I exult in the joy
at sharing the lot
of those who walk along with lowered eyes.

Even now—when the seventeenth of April
is about to join the pile, and my position
could be called one of weakness—
I feel that my sick joints
and the tiger's coat on a sheep's body
herald a greater freedom,
maybe that of truth torn out bit by bit
also because they never tell the whole truth
to a woman, and if she tells it herself
they shut her out from jobs,

ma un essere come me, ad esempio, vi rientra
per via di uno scoppio di risa
o di una esclamazione che coglie di sorpresa,
o per via di un disturbo di salute
che per un intero giorno mi costringe a pensare
alla verità pluriforme—come il botanico
esaltato di fronte a foglie
afferra molte cose del labirinto.

DOBBIAMO LIBERARCI OGGI

La casa paterna è crollata
con tutte le ex-suppellettili vitali
liberati ma non liberi
usciti da lei

non come il sangue dalla vena
e senza particolari rimpianti
che avrebbero dovuto pur esserci
almeno lo pensavamo al momento
di minare la mura
   per questo
   per questa assenza di blandi scontati rimorsi
   per questo rapporto innaturale
   il gelo che ci penetra
   (dato che Edipo ha pur sempre bisogno
   del suo rimorso per essere se stesso
   e liberarsi da Edipo
      in verità questo è l'ultimo alibi
      prima di rinascere
      abbiatene pietà è una grande cosa
      questa difesa del cuore
      questo suo indurimento
      questa strana naturalezza
      che forse è anche menomazione
      che dura che deve durare un attimo soltanto)

Esce la luna dalla nube ritornano le strade
fa già giorno è già domani
che non venga domani il nuovo giorno senza di noi
che dobbiamo liberarci oggi
e non possiamo più improvvisare.

but a being like me, for example, gets in again
through a burst of laughter
or an exclamation that takes people by surprise,
or by a health problem
that for a whole day forces me to think
of multifaceted truth—as the botanist,
ecstatic in front of leaves,
grasps many things of the labyrinth.

IDA VALLERUGO   (1943–)

WE MUST FREE OURSELVES TODAY

The paternal house has collapsed
with all its vital ex-furnishings
freed but not free
gone from it

not like blood from the vein
and without any special regrets
that still should have been there
at least we thought so when
we mined the wall
  on account of this
  on account of this absence of bland predictable remorse
  on account of this unnatural relationship
  the chill that penetrates us
  (given that Oedipus still always needs
  his remorse in order to be himself
  and free himself from Oedipus
    indeed this is the final alibi
    before rebirth
    take pity on it it is a great thing
    this heart's defense
    this hardening of the heart
    this strange naturalness
    that perhaps is also diminution
    that lasts that must last only an instant)

The moon comes out from the cloud the streets return
it is already day it is already tomorrow
let not tomorrow the new day come without us
who must free ourselves today
and can improvise no longer.

ELOISA

E pensare che quello che ti
chiedo è ben poco,
e per te facilissimo!
                    Eloisa a Abelardo
                    Lettera 2ª

I

Qui dimora l'intero e tu disperso
ci ragioni. Che io canti, piú buia
sordidamente, ombra piú pesante
del marmo che mi riposa non conta.
Una sola rondine non mi ti rende
la stagione perduta
e io troppo tempo ho abitato in te
come la ragnatela in un tronco morto

al limite di una terra promessa
non cogliendomi (fu soltanto evocazione
addestramento allo stupro
il fantastico frutto dell'occidente)
mi hai nominata piú bianca della luce
nido di un'idea intricata, torpida fantasia,
pupilla cieca del tuo occhio.

Si sfilava il sibilo dalla teoria lunga
delle stanze: davanti alla porta chiusa
sarò la sorella di quei meli che fuori
si spogliano lisciando a sangue i sensi
e solo la sera ne spegne il tocco.
Un triangolo è divino quando ogni punta è Dio
e ogni lato un'esca. Non c'è veglia piú amara
per me che sono lontano dalla festa.

Le parole non ti costavano molto, ricordi?
scivolano via per filo e per segno
come canoe fluiscono sul filo della corrente.
Non c'era rapida che ne scuotesse il corso
scorresse anche fino al mare il discorso
del tuo sogno soltanto noi ne scontavamo il costo.

Ma subito potessi smemorarmi
annottassero ovunque le pupille degli uomini desti
in un mondo di dormienti
un bestiario delicatamente miniato dallo stilo di chi può

BIANCAMARIA FRABOTTA   (1946–)

HELOISE

*And to think that what I ask of you is
very little,
and for you very easy!*

*Heloise to Abelard
2nd letter*

I
The entirety dwells here and you, distantly,
weigh it. That I, the darker one, chant
sordidly, a shadow heavier
than the marble where I rest does not count.
One lone robin does not bring you back or
summers lost for me
and I have lived too long in you
like the spider's web in a dead trunk

at the border of a promised land
without grasping me (the fantastic fruit of the Occident
was only evocation
training for rape)
you named me whiter than light
the nest of an intricate idea, a torpid fantasy,
blind pupil of your eye.

The hissing unraveled from the long procession
of chambers: before the closed door
I shall be the sister of the apple trees which
outside strip themselves smoothing the senses
raw and only evening dims their touch.
A triangle is divine when each point is God
and each side bait. There is no vigil more bitter
for me, since I am far from the feast.

Words cost you little, remember?
they slip away thoroughly
they flow like canoes on the current's stream.
No rapids could have shaken the course
the discourse was to run to the open sea,
we alone paid the price of your dream.

If only memory would lapse in me
if only the pupils of wakeful men
would turn to night in a world of sleepers
in a bestiary illuminated by the delicate, by the able hand

almeno fin quando arriverò
placida onda di lago a lambirti
i piedi di umide e molli zolle di prato
almeno fin là dove arriva l'essere
e il chierico si fa pierrot
la canaglia un'ariosa città
ogni passante un amico, un evento
allora
l'acqua coprirà il prato e ogni traccia di nome.

SUI PASSATI PROSSIMI E REMOTI

Sui passati prossimi e remoti
ti allarghi a dar ombra
alla mia angustia. Schiacci
viole e ciclamini. Se ci fossero.
Irriconoscibili anche per te che
da non comoda ma eletta altura
mi scruti, fai uso di binocolo,
le parti che giocano e si
scambiano le parti, il disagio
del gruppo che si sbanda, il
collettivo del disagio che al
martedí si riunisce per studiare
le forme storiche della famiglia.
Stabiliamo di fuggire la polvere nera del centro.
Squilla il corno di osso e di bronzo.
È un omaggio alla vecchia poesia.
Sto per prometterti, amore
un'assoluta assenza di requie domenicale.

at least until I, a placid wave in a lake,
come to lap your feet,
the supple, watered furrows of your field
at least to the reaches of being
where the acolyte turns into Pierrot
the rabble an airy city
each passerby a friend, an event
then
the water will cover the field and every trace of a name.

—*Keala Jane Jewell*

YOU ENLARGE ON NEAR AND DISTANT

You enlarge on near and distant
pasts to shade
my anguish. You crush
violets and cyclamens. If there were any.
Undistinguishable even to you, who
from a select if inconvenient knoll
wield binoculars to scrutinize me,
the sides which play and
change sides, the uneasiness
of the group which disbands, the caucus
of the not comfortable which meets
on Tuesdays to study
historical family forms.
We arrange to flee downtown's black grime.
The bone and bronze horn resounds.
It pays homage to the old poetry.
I am about to promise you, love,
an absolute absence of Sunday repose.

—*Keala Jane Jewell*

PREVISIONI DEL TEMPO

non è la Musa della Poesia
è il tuo bel Muso di Poeta
che mi ispira

Su tutte le regioni d'Italia prevedo
cielo coperto o molto nuvoloso
con possibilità di schiarite a San Siro
e locali rovesci verso Viale Argonne quando
tu uscirai a prendere il tram.

Poi prevedo che per una settimana pioverà la pioggia
e se la grata è piena di foglie
entrerà acqua nello scantinato
e si bagneranno i giornali.
Nei fiumi i pesci saranno contenti tu
correrai a ripararti sotto al cappello
per evitare che ti piova sugli occhiali.

Sulle Alpi invece precipitazioni nevose
e nevicherà la neve anche sul Monte Stella a Milano
dove i bambini slittano sui sacchi vuoti dei rifiuti
forse non li hai mai visti.

Poi urlerà il vento e fischierà la bufera
noi due staremo al calduccio sotto le coperte
a sentire i lupi che grattano l'uscio
staremo vicini vicini
(ai rispettivi coniugi).

E chicchi di grandine grossi come uova
picchieranno sui tetti delle 127
e sulle povere vigne.
Come bestemmieresti se tu fossi contadino.

Nei mari molto mossi o localmente agitati
i pesci balleranno
sotto i piedi salati e stanchi
dei poveri pescatori
sorpresi al largo da venti
provenienti come te da nord-est.

Ma poi lo so già tornerà a splendere il sole
sui petti rossi dei pettirossi
sulle lenti degli occhiali miei e tuoi

VIVIAN LAMARQUE   (1946–)

WEATHER FORECAST

it's not Poetry's Muse
but your handsome Poet's Muzzle
that inspires me

Over all regions of Italy I predict
skies overcast or very cloudy
with possibility of clear intervals at San Siro
and local heavy showers around Viale Argonne when
you come out to catch the tram.

Then I predict that the rain will rain for a week
and if the grating is full of leaves
the water will come into the basement
and the newspapers will get wet.
In the rivers the fish will be happy you
will run for shelter under your hat
to avoid having your glasses rained on.

Over the Alps on the other hand precipitations of snow
and the snow will also snow on Monte Stella at Milan
where the children will slide on empty garbage bags
perhaps you have never seen them.

The wind will howl and the storm will whistle
the two of us will stay in the warm under the covers
listening to the wolves scratching at the door
we shall stay very close
(to our respective spouses).

And hailstones as big as eggs
will bang on the roofs of our Fiats
and on the poor vines.
How you would swear if you were a farmer.

In very rough seas or locally disturbed waters
the fish will dance
under the salty and tired feet
of poor fishermen
surprised off-shore by the winds
coming like you from the northeast.

But then I know the sun will come back to shine again
on the red breasts of the robin-redbreasts
on the lenses of our glasses yours and mine

sui parabrezza delle automobili
e in curva abbasseremo tutti insieme i parasole
con una mano.

Banchi locali di nebbia in Val Padana
e in Via Gaetano Moretti 21
dove la facciata della mia casa
che la padrona da vent'anni non vuole rifare
resterà nel vago e ci guadagnerà.
Se mi verrai a trovare ti perderai
farò annusare un tuo verso al mio cane
e partiremo a cercarti.

Ancora una settimana di piogge
che dalle parti di Viale Argonne
assumeranno carattere temporalesco
e tu per i tuoni
ti tapperai le orecchie.

Ma verso sera rosso di sera bel tempo si spera
e io uscirò come una gallina
a guardare l'arcobaleno
(sopra il tetto della tua casa).

E infatti domani lo so tornerà a splendere il sole
e tu andrai a spasso a nord-est di Milano
con la tua famiglia
e io a nord-ovest
con mia figlia.

NON HO SEME DA SPARGERE PER IL MONDO

Non ho seme da spargere per il mondo
non posso inondare i pisciatoi né
i materassi. Il mio avaro seme di donna
è troppo poco per offendere. Cosa posso
lasciare nelle strade nelle case
nei ventri infecondati? Le parole
quelle moltissime
ma già non mi assomigliano più
hanno dimenticato la furia
e la maledizione, sono diventate signorine
un po' malfamate forse
ma sempre signorine.

on the windshields of cars
and on the curve we shall all pull down our shades together
with one hand.

Local banks of fog in Val Padana
and at 21 Via Gaetano Moretti
where the front of my house
which my landlady has been unwilling to do over for twenty years
will remain in the mist and will look better.
If you come to find me you will get lost
I shall have my dog smell one of your poems
and we shall go and look for you.

Another week of rain that in parts of the Viale Argonne
will take on a stormy character
and you during the thunder
will stop your ears.

But towards evening red at night shepherds' delight
and I shall go out like a hen
to look at the rainbow
(over the roof of your house).

And in fact tomorrow I know the sun will shine again
and you will go for a walk northeast of Milan
with your family
and I to the northwest
with my daughter.

PATRIZIA CAVALLI   (1947–)

I HAVE NO SEED TO SCATTER THROUGH THE WORLD

I have no seed to scatter through the world
I cannot flood urinals or
mattresses. My scanty female seed
is too little to give offense. What can I
leave in streets in houses
in unfertilized wombs? Words
multitudes of them
but already they bear no resemblance to me
they have forgotten the rage
and the cursing, they have become young ladies
a little ill-famed perhaps
but still young ladies.

QUANTE TENTAZIONI ATTRAVERSO

Quante tentazioni attraverso
nel percorso tra la camera
e la cucina, tra la cucina
e il cesso. Una macchia
sul muro, un pezzo di carta
caduto in terra, un bicchiere d'acqua,
un guardar dalla finestra,
ciao alla vicina,
una carezza alla gattina.

Così dimentico sempre
l'idea principale, mi perdo
per strada, mi scompongo
giorno per giorno ed è vano
tentare qualsiasi ritorno.

HAI APERTO UNA PORTA

Non so dire perché,
mia compiuta,
hai aperto una porta
nell'aria
della mia reclusione,
né perché mi fai vivere
questi giorni
con gioia magnetica,
con pienezza
lucida e reale.
Forse perché
hai labbra d'amaranto
e dita di biancospino,
perché hai pesche
sulla pelle e mele
nel sangue
o rose per capelli.

HOW MANY TEMPTATIONS I PASS THROUGH

How many temptations I pass through
crossing between the bedroom
and the kitchen, between the kitchen
and the toilet. A spot
on the wall, a piece of paper
fallen on the floor, a glass of water,
a glance out the window,
hi to the neighbor,
a pat for the kitten.

And so I always forget
the main idea, I lose
my way, I get upset
day after day and it's useless
to attempt any kind of return.

MARIANNA FIORE   (1948–)

YOU OPENED A DOOR

I don't know how to say why,
my complete friend,
you have opened a door
in the air
of my seclusion,
nor why you make me live
these days
with magnetic joy,
with a fullness
lucid and true.
Perhaps because
you have lips of amaranth
and fingers of hawthorn,
because you have peaches
on your skin and honey
in your blood
or roses for hair.

So solo
che questo Aprile
porta doni eccessivi
di albe immense
e notti insonni,
accumula terra, fuoco e acqua
e regala tigli
ridondanti
un profumo intenso.
Vorrei
che tu non ricevessi
solo fiori
da me,
ma avessi per te
piante con radici e frutta.
Ti prego arrestami
negli aghi
della tua fantasia,
accoglimi
nel campo di fuoco,
nel rosso clamore
di pace e panico
e colmami
di bellezza e di furore:
io sono l'ape
della tua dimensione.

QUESTA RABBIA

Non ti dico fino a sette
ma fino a settanta volte sette
Matteo, XVIII, 222

Questa rabbia non viene suscitata
da riflessi o simili; sarebbe troppo facile
far nascere robot sotto
lo pseudonimo di uomini, non ci sarebbero
più donne incinte, da esporre come
simbolo di sopravvivenza;

I only know
that this April
brings excessive gifts
of vast dawns
and sleepless nights,
heaps up earth, fire and water
and bestows lindens
overflowing with
an intense perfume.
I should like
you to receive
not only flowers
from me,
but have for your own
plants with roots and fruit.
I beg you make me stay
in the needles
of your fantasy,
receive me
in the field of fire,
in the red clamor
of peace and panic
and fill me
with beauty and frenzy:
I am the bee
of your dimension.

SILVIA BATISTI   (1949–)

THIS RAGE

*I say not unto thee until seven
times but until seventy times seven*
             Matthew, XVIII, 22

This rage is not aroused
by reflections or such; it would be too easy
to give birth to robots under
the pseudonym of men, there would be
no more pregnant women, to be displayed as
symbols of survival;

non ci sarebbe nessuno a cui dare
il cambio, ma solo sport futili,
come sparare o bombardare città.
Ma si sbaglia chi crede
che lo spazio sia limitato alla conoscenza,
e il corpo—usato dai geni come cavia—
solo oggetto, con semplici funzioni
vegetative; l'uomo è materia
combustibile, che brucia con onore
in qualsiasi piazza.

CRONACA

Che vuoi che dica
del tuo matrimonio
Di molte cose ormai
non dico niente
Tu eri bella
come in tanti altri sogni
e bello il tuo sposo
Noi guardavamo da fuori
come profane
Che vuoi che dica
che non ti ho creduta?
Lieve
il mio fantasma bianco
mi sorride ancora
ma ormai lo ignoro
Io curo i miei gatti
e a volte per errore
li confronto con gli altri bambini.

there would be nobody to substitute
for us, but only futile sports
like shooting or bombing cities.
But he is mistaken who thinks
that space is limited to consciousness,
and the body—used as a guinea pig by the genes—
only an object, with simple vegetative
functions; man is combustible
material that burns with honor
in any old piazza.

LORETTA MERENDA   (1950–)

LOCAL NEWS

What do you want me to say
about your marriage
At this point I say nothing
about a lot of things
You were beautiful
as in so many other dreams
and your husband was beautiful
We looked on from the outside
like the profane
What do you want me to say
that I did not believe you?
Easy
my white phantasm
still smiles at me
but from now on I ignore it
I take care of my cats
and sometimes by mistake
compare them with the other children.

IL GIURAMENTO

Scambiamoci questa notte
i dolci doni dell'intimità
che un pegno sono dell'eternità.

Consumiamo lenti e beati
il giuramento sacro del piacere
tra le pieghe gloriose del corpo.

All'alba ci separeremo.

LA MORTE DELLA POESIA

dolci poesie
che ricamavano
bellissime emozioni
che mi portavano
lente e musicali
in atmosfere viola
nella magia
delle cose senza storia
il vostro tempo è finito—
sono morta
piano piano
insieme a voi—
immobile
e zitta
sono rimasta sospesa
in una morte non immobile
ma neanche apparente
ho viaggiato
in una bara
dentro al mio corpo
ho conosciuto
i fiumi mestruali
i contatti nervosi
dello stomaco

GABRIELLA SICA   (1950–)

OATH

Let us exchange tonight
the sweet gifts of intimacy
that are a pledge of eternity.

Slowly, blessedly let us fulfill
the sacred oath of pleasure
between the glorious folds of the body.

At dawn we shall part.

LIVIA CANDIANI   (1952–)

THE DEATH OF POETRY

sweet poems
that embroidered
finest feelings
that slowly musically
carried me away
into violet air
into the magic
of things without history
your time is over—
i am dead
quietly quietly
together with you—
motionless
and silent
I have remained suspended
in a death not motionless
but not apparent either
I have traveled
on a bier
inside my body
I have known
the menstrual rivers
the nervous contacts
of the stomach

gli antri abbandonati
dell'intestino
e ho avuto
ancora
fame di parole emotive
magari meno dolci
ma più sanguigne
intestinali
uterine—
sul mio carro funebre
sono passata
dal mio cervello
l'ho visto gonfio
di idee stracciate
eppure lucidissime
e ho visto
lunghe file
di specchi
in cui lui si rifletteva
e discuteva
con le immagini di sé
che gli davano sempre ragione
e ho visto
i suoi occhi
diventati ciechi
ribaltarsi all'indietro
per vedere solo se stesso
e mostrare al resto
una bianca
stupida
apparenza ferma
razionale—
e sono stata per le strade
e ho visto
tanta gente
tutta con quello stesso
sguardo bianco
idiota
e perfetto
senza urti
lo sguardo cerebrale—
e ho sentito
le urla grige
che escono da ogni carcere
e ho visto gli occhi

the deserted caves
of the intestines
and I have been
still
hungry for emotive words
perhaps less sweet
but more bloody
intestinal
uterine—
on my funeral car
I have passed
out of my brain
I have seen it swollen
with tattered
but most lucid ideas
and have seen
long rows
of mirrors
in which it reflected itself
and conversed
with its own images
that said it was always right
and I have seen
its eyes
having become blind
turn themselves backwards
to see only itself
and show to the rest
a blank
stupid
rational firm
appearance—
and I have been in the streets
and have seen
so many people
all with that same
blank look
idiotic
and perfect
without conflicts
the cerebral look—
and I have heard
the grey howls
that issue from every prison
and have seen the eyes

di ogni carcerato
non più bianchi
ma rossi
stanchi
forti
vitali
occhi che hanno viaggiato
dentro e fuori
di loro—
e ho sentito
il cigolare
e poi il lento
ma sicuro spezzarsi
delle catene femminili
e sulle loro facce
nessuna immagine riflessa
e nella loro voce
i discorsi di un cervello
e la musica di un corpo—
e sono stata nelle piazze
nelle case
nelle scuole
nei prati
e nei boschi
e ho visto
in mezzo a
mucchi di cadaveri
e di moribondi
che barcollavano urlando
ho visto gente
e bella
camminare
con le mani legate
e la bocca imbavagliata
e a ogni passo
la catena ai loro polsi
si macchiava di sangue
ma si consumava
e il bavaglio sulle loro bocche
era sporco di bile
ma scendeva—
lentamente
la mia bara si è aperta
la mia morte
ha smesso di viaggiare

of every prisoner
no longer blank
but red
tired
strong
vital
eyes that have traveled
inside and outside
them—
and I have heard
the clattering
and then the slow
but sure breaking
of women's chains
and on their faces
no image reflected
and in their voice
the discourses of one brain
and the music of one body—
and I have been in the piazzas
in the houses
in the schools
in the fields
and in the woods
and I have seen
in the midst of
heaps of corpses
and of the dying
who staggered howling
I have seen people
beautiful people
walking
with bound hands
and gagged mouths
and at every step
the chains on their wrists
were flecked with blood
but they were wearing out
and the gag on their mouths
was foul with bile
but it was coming undone—
slowly
my bier opened
my death
stopped traveling

e io sono uscita
da una nuova placenta
più grossa e pesante
la placenta storica
e ho cominciato a gridare
col rosso della mia rabbia

LA POETESSA

La poetessa ha capi di parole
fili che frasi smaglia
inusitati paragoni
tra i bagliori
di una cucina economica.
All'eterno ci arriva
per piccoli
disvelamenti,
l'infinito è il rubinetto
a perdere, la fila
dei vuoti a rendere.
La poetessa trama arazzi
in un soggiorno sedizioso:
di notte, tiene una tazza calda
per i mostri, là, sul pianerottolo.
Bisogna esser gentili—lei dice.
Bisogna esser riservati: mai che ti sbatta in faccia
il suo piede-feticcio
mai che ti porga
la sua larga piaga da leccare.
Il sangue è rosso perché tu lo veda.
Ma lei lo sa
che dalla porta di Duchamp non può passare.
Le sue pantofole, al massimo
saran le quattro piume di una starlet:
ammiccanti
dalla sporta del latte, una rivolta di Gulliver.
A lei tocca ancora
contare i bossoli nella pistola
assicurarsi che tutto sia in ordine,
contabile fino in questo odioso mestiere.

and I have emerged
from a larger and heavier
new placenta
the historic placenta
and have begun to scream
with the redness of my rage

MARTA FABIANI (1953–)

THE POETESS

The poetess has paragraphs of words
threads she unravels as phrases
unusual comparisons
among the gleams
of a kitchen stove.
She reaches the eternal
by little
unveilings,
the infinite is the leaking
faucet, the row
of empties to return.
The poetess weaves tapestries
in a seditious lodging:
at night she keeps a warm cup
for the monsters, there, on the landing.
We must be nice, she says.
We must be discreet so that she never hurls in your face
her foot fetish
never offers you
her great sore to lick.
Blood is red so that you may see it.
But she knows
that she cannot pass through Duchamp's door.
Her slippers, at most,
will be the four feathers of a starlet:
winking
from the shopping bag of milk cartons, a Gulliver's revolt.
It is still her job
to count the chambers in the pistol
to be sure everything is in order,
accountant even in this hateful occupation.

Sibilla Aleramo (Rina Faccio) (1876–1960)
Born in Alessandria in the Piedmont, Rina Faccio was raped when she was fifteen by an employee in the factory where her father worked. She married the employee because she became pregnant by him; the marriage was made miserable by the husband's brutal jealousy. Faccio found an outlet in writing short stories (in the style of Gabriele D'Annunzio) and articles for provincial newspapers. After 1898 these articles expressed inreasing concern with feminist issues. In 1902 she left her husband and child, went to Rome, and changed her name to Sibilla Aleramo. She lived for seven years with Giovanni Cena, a poet and novelist, who encouraged her to write her own story in *Una donna* (1906). This novel was an international success. During this period Aleramo worked to alleviate the appalling living conditions of Roman workers. After 1910 she had numerous love affairs, many with contemporary poets, among whom was Dino Campana. Aleramo wrote several more novels and, in 1921, began to publish poetry. The poetry was collected into one edition, *Selva d'amore*, published in 1947. In the same year her correspondence with Dino Campana was published as *Lettere*. She died in Rome.

Anonymous (Thirteenth Century)
Italian began to develop as a literary language in the thirteenth century. It was a direct descendant of medieval Latin culture, both classical and clerical, but its lyric inspiration was drawn from two auxiliary sources. One was popular oral tradition—the ballads, love songs, laments, and dance and hunting songs sung by people at work and play. The other source was the poetry of courtly love that had developed in twelfth-century Provence. This poetry was brought to Italy by troubadours traveling in the North and composing in Provençal, and by Sicilian poets at the court of Frederick II of Hohenstaufen in the South. The language was strongly regional, and it was not until the center of culture moved to Tuscany in the second half of the century that Tuscan became the literary language and the one that evolved into modern standard Italian.

The sonnet first took form at Frederick's court. The octave of lines of eleven syllables had alternating rhymes (ABABABAB), while the sestet rhymed CDCDCD or CDECDE. We know little about the authors except what the poems themselves tell us. We may assume that the first one in this volume was written by a woman, a member of the landed nobility or gentry who practiced falconry as a sport, and that she was sufficiently educated or "accomplished" to write a sonnet—although perhaps not as perfectly as La Compiuta Donzella.

Anonymous Popular Songs
(Late Nineteenth and Early Twentieth Centuries)
Many popular songs of the late nineteenth and early twentieth centuries expressed women's resentment of their exploitation as wives and workers. Included here are three songs from Tuscany, two lullabies and the lament of a disillusioned wife; one song of Venetian silk-spinners; and one of rice-field workers. The latter was used in the film *Bitter Rice* (*Riso amaro*).

Silvia Batisti (1949–)
Silvia Batisti was born in Greve in Chianti, near Florence. Self-taught, she has worked as a hairdresser, metal worker, typesetter, and proofreader. Now she is an archivist, and lives in Antonella, near Florence. She works for a number of journals, including *Salvo imprevisti*, a quarterly of poetry and other documents of struggle. Batisti has published two volumes of verse, *Di pari passo* (1971) and *Costruzione per un delirio* (1975).

Mariella Bettarini (1942–)
Mariella Bettarini was born in Florence, where she now lives and teaches elementary school. She has published eight books of poetry: *Il pudore e l'effondersi* (1966); *La rivoluzione copernicana* (1970); *Terra di tutti e altre poesie* (1972); *Dal vero* (1974); *In bocca alla balena* (1977); *Diario fiorentino* (1979); *Trittico per Pasolini* (1979); and *Ossessi oggetti/spiritate materie* (1981). She has also edited works on feminism, translated works by Simone Weil into Italian, and now, along with Silvia Batisti, directs *Salvo imprevisti*, which she helped to found in 1974.

Caterina Bon Brenzoni (1813–1856)
Caterina Bon Brenzoni was born in Verona. Her father, Count Bon, died while she was still young, and at eighteen she married Count Brenzoni. She lived in constant poor health and suffered the deaths of her two infant sons. When she was thirty-five she met Mary Somerville, a Scottish woman learned in astronomy who had translated the Marquis de Laplace's *Mécanique céleste*, popularizing it under the title *The Mechanism of the Heavens* (1831). This work inspired Brenzoni to write *I cieli* (1851), which expresses her enthusiastic interest in astronomy.

Livia Candiani (1952–)
Livia Candiani was born in Milan. She is a student of philosophy and has taken part in feminist collectives.

Franca Maria Catri (1931–)
Franca Maria Catri was born in Rome where she currently lives and works as a medical doctor. Her poetry has appeared in various magazines and anthologies.

Liana Catri (1929–)
Liana Catri was born in Rome and now lives in Riana. She has published two collections of poetry, *La grande favola* and *La fatica di essere donna*. She is a member of an artisans' collective called *Le rospe nere*.

Patrizia Cavalli (1947–)
Patrizia Cavalli was born in Todi. Now she lives in Rome where she completed an advanced degree in arts with a thesis on the aesthetics of music. Her poems have appeared in the journals *Paragone* and *Nuovi argomenti*. Her first volume of poetry, *Le mie poesie non cambieranno il mondo*, was published in 1974, and her second, *Il cielo*, in 1981.

Giuseppina Turrisi Colonna (1822–1848)
Giuseppina Turrisi Colonna was born of a noble Sicilian family in Palermo. In 1847 she married Giuseppe de Spuches, Prince of Galati, who was also a poet. Colonna began to write early, on patriotic and romantic themes, and won recognition for her poems although she died young.

Vittoria Colonna (1490–1547)
Vittoria Colonna, daughter of the Grand Constable of Naples, was born near Rome. At the insistence of the King of Naples, she was betrothed at the age of four to Ferrante d'Avalos, Marquis of Pescara. She was well educated and early showed a talent for writing. Colonna had many suitors, but married d'Avalos by her own wish when she was nineteen.

The couple had two happy years on the island of Ischia in the Bay of Naples. But these years fell in the period when Italy was subject to constant invasion and partition by France, Spain, and the German empire. D'Avalos supported Spain (which had established the kingdom of Naples) and in 1511 joined the league against the French; he was taken prisoner at the battle of Ravenna in 1512. During the months of detention and years of campaigning that followed, he and Colonna were seldom together, but they carried on a correspondence in both prose and verse. After the defeat of France at Pavia, in 1525, the anti-imperialists tried to win d'Avalos to their side by offering him the crown of Naples; Colonna's influence helped to keep him loyal to the emperor, the Spanish Charles V. Later that year d'Avalos was wounded and died in Milan before Colonna could reach him. She retired to Ischia where her grief and love for her husband found expression in her sonnets.

Colonna visited Rome several times and spent the last three years of her life there. She remained a widow and had many friends and admirers among popes, princes, scholars, and artists. The most famous of these was Michelangelo, who dedicated some of his finest sonnets to her. A collection of her poems, which appeared in 1538, was the first volume of poetry by a woman to be published in Italy. Four more editions appeared in 1539 and another fourteen in 1540. Colonna's work was part of the flowering of women's poetry in mid-sixteenth-century Italy and is evidence of the position upper-class women sometimes attained in the literary and court society of that period.

La Compiuta Donzella (Thirteenth Century)
Her title, "The Accomplished Maiden," is almost all we know about this poet. She lived in Florence in the second half of the thirteenth century, and only three poems attributed to her are extant. She was a contemporary of the young Dante (who wrote *La vita nuova* in 1292 and 1293) and the emerging school of lyric poets. Guittone d'Arezzo, one of the first poets of the *Stil nuovo*, admired her work.

La Contessa Lara (Eva Cattermole Mancini) (1849–1896)
Eva Cattermole was the daughter of a Russian father and an English mother. She learned languages from her father and music from her mother. Her early life was spent in Florence where she frequented the literary salons and published her first poems, *Canti e ghirlandi*, in 1867. She married Francesco Mancini, an official in the *Bersaglieri*, and went with him to his various posts in Rome, Naples, and Milan. In Milan she had an affair with Giuseppe Bennati, whom her husband killed in a duel. Eva left Mancini, returned to Florence, and worked on the newspaper *Fieramosca*. In 1883, she published her second, very successful volume of poetry, *Versi*, under the pseudonym La Contessa Lara, and continued to write poems, stories, and articles for many different papers and periodicals. One of her columns was entitled "Cronache femminile" ("Women's News"). After her third volume of poems (*E ancora versi*, 1886) she wrote mainly prose—short stories, novels, and children's stories. Her death was violent: the painter Pierantoni, with whom she was living, killed her.

Marta Fabiani (1953–)
Marta Fabiani was born in Pavia and now lives in Milan. She is a freelance writer. A collection of her poems, *Maratona*, has been published by a writers' cooperative called *Cooperativa scrittori*. She has edited Sylvia Plath's letters to her mother and has directed a series of radio plays in Switzerland.

Marianna Fiore (1948–)
Marianna Fiore was born in Ancona. She is a biologist and works in a health clinic for women. As is apparent in the Italian, the "complete friend" in *"Hai aperto una porta"* (*"You Opened a Door"*) is a woman.

Biancamaria Frabotta (1946–)

Born in Rome, Biancamaria Frabotta now teaches Italian literature at the university there. Her poetry and articles have appeared in the journal *Manifesto* as well as in other journals and newspapers. She is the editor of several books on feminism, including *Femminismo e la lotta di classe in Italia (Feminism and Class Struggle in Italy)*, *La politica del femminismo (The Politics of Feminism)*, and the anthology of Italian women's poetry *Donne in Poesia (Women in Poetry)*. Frabotta recently published a full-length study of feminist literature entitled *Letteratura al femminile* (1980). Her volumes of poetry are: *Affemminata* (1977), *Il rumore bianco* (1982), and *Appunti di volo* (1985).

Veronica Franco (1546–1591)

Veronica Franco was born in Venice and became one of the most famous of a group of courtesans described as "honest" because of their high rank and cultural gifts. She was loved and admired by princes and intellectuals; her portrait was painted by Tintoretto. She met Henry III of Valois on his way to receive the French crown in 1574, gave him her miniature, and dedicated two sonnets to him. She exchanged uninhibited erotic verse with the poet Maffio Venier who had criticized her poetry and who she thought was Marco Venier. Franco wrote mainly in terza rima. The first edition of her collected poems, *Terze Rime*, dedicated to the Duke of Mantua, was published in 1575. After 1580, Franco apparently renounced her life in society and devoted herself to religious work.

Luciana Frezza (1926–)

Luciana Frezza was born in Rome. She studied with Giuseppe Ungaretti and under his supervision wrote a thesis on Eugenio Montale. Now living in Rome, Frezza devotes herself to translating various French poets of the late nineteenth century including Mallarmé, Jules Laforgue, G. Nouveau, and Verlaine. She is also compiling an anthology of Jean-Paul Fargue's poetry. Her four volumes of poetry, which appeared between 1954 and 1971, include *Un tempo di speranza* (1971) (*A Time of Hope*), in which "Requiem for Sylvia Plath" first appeared, as well as *Cefalù e altre poesia* (1958), *La farfalla e la rosa* (1962), and *Cara Milano* (1967).

Erminia Fua Fusinato (1834–1876)

Erminia Fua was born of Jewish parents in Rovigo. She began to write early and was encouraged to publish her first poems in 1852 by the poet Fusinato, a widower, whom she married in 1856. When her husband had problems in business, she became a teacher. In 1871 she taught Italian at the Scuola Normale in Rome and later directed the Scuola Superiore Femminile, also in Rome. In addition to her poetry (published in 1853 and 1874), Fusinato wrote about education (*Scritti educativi*, 1873). She believed women should be allowed time away from domestic duties to study literature.

Veronica Gambara (1485–1550)

Veronica Gambara was born in Pratalboino (Brescia) of a noble family, and received a thorough education in Latin, Greek, philosophy, and theology. Such instruction was not unusual for daughters of wealthy or noble families in that period. Gambara and the female poets who followed her benefited from the revolution in manners and education begun by the Italian humanists of the preceding century. Among the most influential of these earlier scholars was Petrarch; his poetry became the model for the succeeding generations of writers. Gambara wrote lyrics and Petrarchan sonnets and corresponded with Tasso, Aretino, and Bembo. She was the wife of Giberto X, Lord of Coreggio; after his death in 1518 she governed Coreggio with skill, even repulsing an armed attack by a neighboring duchy in 1538. Ludovico Ariosto and Titian were guests at her court, as was Emperor Charles V. Gambara died in Coreggio.

Rosanna Guerrini (1935–)

Rosanna Guerrini was born in Milan. In 1957 she abandoned her university studies in ancient literature to move to Rome, where she married. She now divides her time between Rome and Milan and works in both radio and journalism. In 1966 her poetry collection, *Invettive*, was published. All of her subsequent poems, including "To My Children," have appeared in various journals.

Amalia Guglielminetti (1885–1941)

Amalia Guglielminetti was born in Turin. She began to publish poetry at the age of eighteen with *Voci di giovinezza* (1903); *La vergine folle* followed in 1907. Her verse reflects her intolerance of an ordinary or tranquil life, and she became known for her passionate love affairs. The most famous of these was with the writer Guido Gozzano. Their correspondence, published posthumously in 1951, reveals the progress of their affair; it is also a revealing social document of the early twentieth century. An autobiographical and fragmented novel, *Le seduzioni*, was written at the end of the relationship, in 1908. Another book of poetry, *L'insonne*, appeared in 1913. Guglielminetti wrote several other novels, short stories, and dramas for children. She died in Turin.

Margherita Guidacci (1921–)

Margherita Guidacci was born in Florence and later attended the university there. Her thesis on Giuseppe Ungaretti was written under the direction of the critic Giuseppe De Robertis. She now lives in Rome where she teaches English to high school students. She has translated Pound, Eliot, Dickinson, and other writers into Italian. Guidacci has published seven volumes of poetry; her first appeared when she was sixteen years old, and the most recent one is *Neurosuite* (1970).

Armanda Guiducci (1923–)
Born in Naples, Armanda Guiducci studied philosophy at the University of Milan, where she now lives. She has edited and contributed to numerous journals in Italy such as *Ragionamenti, Passato e presente,* and *Tempi moderni.* She has published two volumes of poetry, *Poesie per un'uomo* (1965), from which the first two poems here are selected, and *A colpi di silenzio* (1982). Her critical writings have been numerous and influential: *La Domenica della rivoluzione* (1961); *Dallo zdavonismo allo strutturalismo* (1967); *Il mito pavese* (1965); *Letturi di Pavese* (1972). She entered the feminist debate in 1974 with the book *La mela e il serpente: autoanalisi di una donna.*

Jolanda Insana (1937–)
Jolanda Insana was born in Messina and currently lives in Rome. She has published three volumes of poetry, *Sciarra amara* (1977), *Fendenti fonici* (1982), and *Il Colettam* (1985), for which she won the Rimini Doesia Prize. Her work has appeared in the anthologies *Poesia femminista italiana* (1978), *Poesia degli anni settanta* (1979), and *Versi d'amore* (1982). Insana has also translated works of Sappho and pursues an active career as an artist.

Vivian Lamarque (1946–)
Born in Tesero, and now living in Milan, Vivian Lamarque has contributed poems to *Paragone* and *Nuovi argomenti.* Giovanni Raboni introduced her work to the readers of the former with these remarks: "Lamarque is absolutely original and fairly uncommon, and she has the grace and ingenuity to write poetry as if she were dealing with a form of writing that has nothing to do with literature." Lamarque's 1981 volume, *Teresino,* was awarded the Premio Viareggio for new writers.

Anna Malfaiera (1926–)
Anna Malfaiera, born in Fabriano, studied education at the University of Urbino. For the past twenty years she has lived and worked in Rome, where she left a comfortable position in the Ministry of Public Education for the demanding, but for her less alienating, work of teaching. Malfaiera has written several volumes of poetry and has contributed to journals on art and literature. The poem included here is from *Il vantaggio privato* (1970).

Sandra Mangini (c. 1940–)
The work of Sandra Mangini has been published in various prestigious periodicals, including *Nuovi argomenti, Il menabò* and *Paragone,* where "Ring Road" originally appeared in 1966.

Dacia Maraini (1936–)

Dacia Maraini was born in Florence. She lived in Japan for eight years, two of which were spent in a concentration camp. She now lives in Rome and in the last twenty-three years has written novels, short stories, plays, and poetry and has been active as a journalist. Her first novel, *La vacanza*, appeared in 1961; her second, *L'età del malessere* (1963), was awarded the Formentor international prize. The novel *Donne in guerra* (1978) is adamantly feminist, as are many of her works. Maraini has edited an anthology of modern Japanese poetry, *Cento anni di protesta* (1968), and is an active supporter of the women's theater movement in Rome. Her poetry has been published in two volumes: *Crudeltà all'aria aperta* (1966) and *Donne mie* (1974).

Petronilla Paolini Massimi (1663–1726)

Petronilla Paolini was born in Tagliacozzo and lived most of her life in Rome, where she was educated at the Convent of the Holy Spirit. Her long canzoni express in heroic terms the unhappiness of her life. Her father was assassinated, probably by agents of the Marquis Francesco di Massimi who wished to marry her for the fortune she would inherit. This marriage was forced on her when she was ten by her mother and the Pope, Clement X, a relative of Massimi. After the wedding, the poet lived secluded in the Castel Sant' Angelo, which her husband governed, and where she witnessed *"funeste scene"* ("sad spectacles") of imprisonment and persecution. The building was originally erected as a mausoleum for the emperor Hadrian and was used as a tomb for emperors until the death of Septimus Severus. In Massimi's time it served as a prison.

When Massimi tried to leave the Castel Sant 'Angelo for the convent where her literary education had begun, her husband denied her financial support and refused to let her see her sons even when one was dying. The poet took her case to court and won. The Marquis died in 1709; Massimi remained at the convent for two more years after her husband's death and devoted herself to writing and studying philosophy.

In 1698, Massimi was elected to the Accademia degli Arcadi under the name Fidalma Partenide. Her poems were published in the volumes of *Rime degli Arcadi* (1716–1722).

Chiara Matraini (1514–c.1597)

Chiara Matraini was born in Lucca and when barely seventeen married Vincenzo Contarini. We know little about her life; she was apparently widowed after twenty-five years of marriage and died sometime after 1597, the date of the third printing of her *Rime*, to which she wrote an introduction. When Matraini writes in praise of liberty, she may be thinking less of her personal situation than of the threat to her native Lucca by the Spaniards. She might also be protesting the new despotism of church and state that was a result of the establishment of the Inquisition in Italy in 1540.

Daria Menicanti (1914–)
Daria Menicanti was born in Piacenza. She studied aesthetics at the University of Milan, the city where she now lives and teaches. She has published three books of poetry, *Cittá come* (1964), *Un nero d'ombra* (1969), and *Poesie per un passante* (1978).

Loretta Merenda (1950–)
Loretta Merenda was born in Bagnacavallo and now lives in Ravenna and Bologna. Her degree is in pedagogy and she teaches the sociology of the family at the University of Bologna. She has published *Un filo di seta sottile* (1979), *Saldi* (1980), and *Luoghi comuni* (1981).

Isabella di Morra (1520–1546)
Isabella di Morra was born near Naples. Her father was Giovan Michele di Morra who, in 1528, was accused of betraying the Spanish rulers of Naples to the French and forced to flee to France. The family remained in the isolated *castello* of Favale. There di Morra, encouraged and helped by her tutor, began a correspondence, largely in verse, with a neighboring Spanish nobleman, Diego Sandoval de Castro. When one of her letters was discovered, her brothers killed her, the tutor, and de Castro to avenge the family honor. Her poems were published posthumously.

Ada Negri (1870–1945)
Ada Negri was born in Lodi to an artisan's family. Although she had to struggle for an education, she became a teacher in a village school. Her first book of poems, *Fatalità* (1892), describes the tragic lives of the poor. Her reputation as a poet was confirmed by her second volume, *Tempeste* (1896); this led to her appointment at the Normal School of Milan. In *Maternità* (1910), one of several other volumes of poetry, she wrote of family life. After separating from her husband, she moved to Switzerland and wrote poems of exile and several novels. She died in Milan.

Giulia Niccolai (1934–)
Giulia Niccolai was born in Milan. Because her mother was American and her father Italian, she has lived in both America and Italy. Her first novel, *Il grande angolo* (1966), drew on her ten years of experience as a photographer. Since she was five she has lived in the Italian countryside near Mulino di Bazzano. Niccolai and Adriano Spatola publish a poetry review entitled *Tam Tam. Humpty Dumpty*, a book of "concrete poetry," appeared in 1969, followed by *Greenwich* in 1971. These volumes were originally published with English titles. In 1974 Niccolai published *Poema e Oggetto*, a volume of "visible poetry." A collection of her poems has been translated into English under the title *Substitution* (1975) and the collection *Harry's Bar e altre poesia, 1969–1980* was published in 1981.

Maria Guacci Nobile (1808–1848)

Born and raised in Naples, Maria Guacci married a professor of astronomy there and encouraged a group of poets to frequent their home. She published two volumes of poems, mainly canzoni. In one of these she notes the small role allowed women in civil life; in another, *Alle donne napoletane,* she appeals to a combination of feminine pride in and love for their native city. In an ode to Giambattista Vico, she says she feels unappreciated in her own home just as he was unappreciated in his time and place.

Rossana Ombres (1931–)

Rossana Ombres has published five volumes of poetry, including *Orrizonte anche tu* (1956) and *Bestiario d'amore* (1974), as well as numerous short stories and two novels, including *Principessa Giacinta* (1970). She also writes literary criticism for *La stampa,* an influential newspaper published in her native Turin. She now lives in Rome. Like her contemporary Amelia Rosselli, Ombres translates from English and is much influenced by the Elizabethans. The epigraph for "Nocturne," the poem included here, is the fourth line of John Donne's poem "Aire and Angels," which begins:

Twice or thrice had I loved thee,
  Before I knew thy face or name,
  So in a voice, so in a shapelesse flame...

Piera Oppezzo (1934–)

Piera Oppezzo was born in Turin and has lived in Milan since 1966. She has worked as a seamstress, store clerk, typesetter, and editorial assistant. Oppezzo has published *L'uomo qui presente* (1966), *1967, sì a una reale interruzione* (1976), and *Minuto per minuto* (1978). A militant spokeswoman for feminism, she writes of herself: "Like other women, when confronted by politics, writing or any other activity considered positive, I would like to regenerate myself by returning to nothingness."

Vittoria Aganoor Pompili (1855–1910)

Vittoria Aganoor was born in Padua to an Armenian father and an Italian mother. She had a happy early life and received a good literary education. Later, she experienced an intense and unhappy love affair, which gave a melancholy cast to her lyrics. Aganoor was unwilling to publish her poems because of their private nature. After her father's death she lived in Venice caring for her mother, who finally persuaded her to publish her poetry under the title *Leggenda eterna* (1900). This volume met with great success and was translated into Armenian in 1905. In 1901 Aganoor married Guido Pompili, a lawyer. They lived in Perugia, where the poet became friends with Maria Alinda Bonacci Brunamonti. Together these writers gave Perugia the reputation of being the "realm of the Muses." Vittoria Pompili died after an operation in Rome, and a few hours later her husband committed suicide. Pompili's complete poems, in *Poesie complete*, were published in 1912.

Antonia Pozzi (1912–1938)
Antonia Pozzi, a native of Milan, died at twenty-six without having shown her poetry to anyone except her close friends. Her parents published selections from her notebooks the year after her death under the title *Parole*. The book attracted much attention and several poems from it were translated into French, German, and Rumanian. An expanded edition of her work appeared in 1943 and again in 1948 with an introduction by Eugenio Montale, who likened Pozzi's work to that of Rilke and Ungaretti. Her essay, "Flaubert: The Literary Development," was published in 1940.

Modesta dal Pozzo (1555–1592)
We know very little about Modesta dal Pozzo except that, like Gaspara Stampa and Veronica Franco, she lived in Venice. Dal Pozzo married Filippo dei Georgi (or Zorzi). Volumes of her poetry appeared in 1581, 1582, and 1583, but "Il merito delle donne" was not published until after her death; her daughter brought it out in 1600. Modesta dal Pozzo (meaning "modesty of the well") adopted the transparent pseudonym of Moderata Fonte ("moderate spring" or "fountain").

Amelia Rosselli (1930–)
Amelia Rosselli, daughter of Carlo Rosselli (the antifascist exile who was assassinated along with his brother, Nello, in 1937) and an English mother, was born in Paris. In 1950, after living in France, England, and the United States, she moved to Rome. Roselli is a theoretician and composer of music as well as a translator and essayist. She writes in French, English, and Italian. She came to Italian poetry rather late; an early group of her lyrics was presented by Pasolini when it first appeared in 1963. Her volumes of Italian poetry are: *Variazioni belliche* (1964), *Serie ospedaliera* (1969), *Documento* (1976), and *Primi critti 1952–1963* (1980), and *Impromptu* (1981). In 1981 Rosselli received the Premio Pasolini for her entire opus.

Diodata Saluzzo (1774–1840)
Diodata Saluzzo was born in Turin. Her father, Count Giuseppe Angelo Saluzzo, was one of the founders of the Academy of Sciences at Turin. Her mother, well versed in literature and philosophy, was unusual for one of her rank at that time in that she nursed her children herself and supervised their education. Diodata grew up with five younger brothers in an atmosphere of moral and patriotic fervor characteristic of the Piedmontese nobility loyal to the royal house of Savoy. She would have liked to follow a military career, as her brothers did; instead she wrote on heroic themes.

One of her early poems, "Amazzoni," is an epic of the Amazons in twenty-four cantos. She later wrote a twenty-canto poem, "Ipazia," about Hypatia, the beautiful Neoplatonist of fourth-century Alexandria who was a victim of persecution by the Christians. Saluzzo also wrote many lyrics, two tragedies, and some short stories. In 1799 she married a friend of her father's, Count Roero. She was widowed after three years and returned to her parents' home to help them manage their estates. Among her women friends were Teresa Bandettini, the poet, and Clotide Tambroni, professor of Greek at the University of Bologna. Saluzzo was praised by many contemporary writers, including Vittorio Alfieri, Ugo Foscolo, and Alessandro Manzoni.

Gabriella Sica (1950–)

Gabriella Sica was born in Viterbo and presently lives in Rome, where she participates in the group *"Le scritture"* and contributes to numerous journals. She has published *Sanguineti* (1974), as well as poems and short stories in magazines and anthologies.

Maria Luisa Spaziani (1924–)

A native of Turin, Maria Luisa Sapziani now lives in Rome and teaches French language and literature at the University of Messina. She writes for *La stampa* and appears on Italian and Swiss radio and television. Her wide-ranging translations include seventeenth-century French drama and Cocteau. Her own poetry, which has been translated into thirteen languages and has received many prizes, has been said to show influences of such poets as Montale, Rilke, and Dylan Thomas. Spaziani's volumes of poetry are: *Le acque del sabato* (1954), *Il gong* (1962), *Utilità della memoria* (1966), *L'occhio del ciclone* (1970), *Ultrasuoni* (1976), *Transito con catene* (1977), and *Geometria del disordine* (1981).

Gaspara Stampa (c.1523–1554)

Gaspara Stampa was born in Padua. Her mother was Venetian; her father, a descendent of Milanese nobility, was a jewel merchant and a man who appreciated music and poetry. He saw that his children, Cassandra, Baldassare (also a poet), and Gaspara, were educated not only in the traditional classical studies but also in music and prosody. After his death in 1531, the family moved to Venice where the children's education was continued according to their father's wishes. From 1535 to 1540 the Stampas' home was a cultural center for Venetian artists, musicians, writers, and noblemen.

Gaspara Stampa became a member of the Accademia dei Dubbiosi with the name of Anasilla and lived the free life of a high-ranking "honest" courtesan (see page 138). For three years (1548–1551) she was in love with Count Collaltino di Collalto, to whom many of her poems are dedicated. Her sonnets to the Count express the range and depth of her passion. She writes of joy, fear, jealousy, and disillusion in language that, although it uses established forms and conceits, is intensely personal. When Stampa invokes Death (*la morte:* ''she, who makes pale the world...'') she is following a Petrarchan convention that male poets used to impress upon the women they courted that they were ''dying'' from love. This was part of the game of courtship: Before marriage the bride was supposed to be remote and to hold the power of life or death over her lover. Stampa has reversed this situation—with the added difference that what she felt was real and not an artificial or poetic attitude.

In 1553 Stampa fell sick and the next year died of a fever. Her poems were published posthumously by her sister Cassandra.

Laura Terracina (1519–1577)

Laura Terracina was born in Naples to a noble family loyal to the Spanish ascendancy. Her education followed the classical pattern of the time. For two years (1545–47) she was a member of the Accademia degli Incogniti under the name of Febea, and was in contact with other contemporary poets. Terracina's first volume of poetry, *Rime,* was published in Venice in 1548 and her second in Florence in 1549. *The Discourse on the Principle in All the Cantos of Orlando Furioso,* which also appeared in 1549, further increased her reputation as a poet and a scholar. This poem, the dedication to which is included in this volume, is a commentary in verse on the first forty-six cantos of Ludovico Ariosto's *Orlando Furioso.* It is a tour de force. Each canto has seven stanzas, the last lines of which constitute the first stanza of the corresponding canto in *Orlando Furioso.* Continuing the exhortation of the dedication in canto 38, Terracina reproves women for not studying enough; she encourages them to ''leave their needle, thread, and cloth'' and ''take up the burden of letters,'' and concludes ''Let us leave henceforth this servitude and follow holy blessed literature.''

Ida Vallerugo (1943–)

Ida Vallerugo was born in Medano, Friuli, where she now lives and teaches. In 1968 she published *Il porto dipinto,* in 1970 *La nostra relativa innocenza,* and in 1972 *Interrogatorio.* Vallerugo works in a public library, and although she has been formally educated, she considers herself self-taught.

Annie Vivanti (1868–1942)

Annie Vivanti was born in London. She moved to Bologna as a young woman and there she met Giosué Carducci, who encouraged her to write poetry. They were lovers for a brief period. In 1892 Vivanti married the Irish journalist John Chartres and moved to America with him. During her twenty years of married life Vivanti published nothing and raised her daughter, a child-prodigy violinist. After her husband died, and since her daughter was by then grown, Vivanti moved to Torino. There she wrote prodigiously—novels, poetry, short stories, and essays—until her death A collection of Vivanti's poems, *Lirica*, was published in 1921. Since she was Jewish and a British subject, the last years of her life, under Fascism, were extremely difficult; when she died none of the critics and poets who had praised her work publicly recognized her funeral.

Faustina Maratti Zappi (c. 1680–1745)

Faustina Maratti, born in Rome, was the daughter of the painter Carlo Maratti, whose portrait of her is now in the National Gallery in Rome. Maratti married Giovanni B. F. Zappi, a poet and founder of the academy, Arcadia, to which Faustina was admitted in 1704 under the name Aglauro Cidonia. While a member of the academy she disputed the nature of love with Petronilla Massimi. Arcadia was the poets' refuge from the censorship instituted by the Inquisition in the middle of the sixteenth century. Nothing offensive to papal or civil authority could be printed, and so serious subject matter and deep feeling were replaced or disguised by the artificial conventions of Arcadia. Against such a background, Zappi's sonnet stands out as an expression of personal distress.

The Zappis lived in Rome until 1719 when one of their sons and then Giovanni himself died. Faustina Zappi then moved to Imola and raised her other children.

ACKNOWLEDGMENTS

For permission to reprint or translate the poems in this volume we acknowledge with thanks the following publishers and poets:

ANONYMOUS POPULAR SONGS: "E la mi' mamma," "La malcontenta," "Il lamento della sposa," "O cara mamma vienimi incontra," and "Povere filandine" from *Canti della protesta femminile* ed. by Agata Curra, Giuseppe Vettori, and Rosalba Vinci. Rome: Newton Compton Editori, 1977. Translated by permission of the publisher.

MARIELLA BETTARINI: "Come il botanico" from her volume *La rivoluzione copernica*. Rome: Trevi Editore, 1970. By permission of the poet.

FRANCA MARIA CATRI: "Madre sorella" from *Care donne* ed. by Elia Malago. Forli: Editrice Forum/Quinta Generazione, 1980. By permission of the poet and the publisher.

PATRIZIA CAVALLI: "Non ho seme da spargere per il mondo" and "Quante tentazioni attraverso" from her volume *Le mie poesie non cambieranno il mondo*. Turin: Giulio Einaudi Editore, 1974. By permission of the publisher.

BIANCAMARIA FRABOTTA: "Eloisa" and "Sui passati prossimi e remoti" from her volume *Il rumore bianco*. Milan: Giangiacomo Feltrinelli Editore, 1982. By permission of the poet.

LUCIANNA FREZZA: "Requiem per Sylvia Plath" from her volume *Un tempo di speranza*. Vicenza: Casa Editrice Neri Pozza, 1971. By permission of the publisher.

ROSANNA GUERRINI: "Ai miei figli" from *Nuovi argomenti*, no. 14 (1969). Milan: Garzanti Editore. By permission of the publisher.

MARGHERITA GUIDACCI: "Molte volte novembre è ritornato" from her volume *Poesie*. Milan: Rizzoli Editore, 1965. By permission of the poet and the publisher.

ARMANDA GUIDUCCI: "Uomo" and "Parità" from her volume *Poesie per un uomo*. Milan: Arnoldo Mondadori Editore, 1965. "La canzone del martello" from her volume *A colpi di silenzio*. Milan: Lanfranchi Editore, 1982. By the kind permission of the author.

JOLANDA INSANA: "Perchè non ho voluto chiedere" from *Versi d'amore* ed. by G. M. Loperfido. Venice: Corbo e Fiore Editore, 1982. By permission of the poet and the publisher.

VIVIAN LAMARQUE: "Previsioni del tempo" from her volume *Teresino*. Milan: Guanda Editore, 1981. By permission of the poet.

ANNA MALFAIERA: "Non potrò più ridere di vera allegria" from her volume *Il vantaggio privato*. Caltanisseta: Casa Editrice Salvatore Sciascia, 1970. By permission of the publisher.

SANDRA MANGINI: "Raccordo anulare" from *Paragone*, no. 194 (1966). Florence: G.C. Sansoni Editore. By permission of the publisher.

DACIA MARAINI: "Le poesie delle donne" from her volume *Donne mie*. Turin: Giulio Einaudi Editore, 1974. By permission of the publisher. "Madre Canina" from her volume *Crudeltà all'aria aperta*. Milan: Giangiacomo Feltrinelli Editore, 1966. By permission of the poet.

MENICANTI, DARIA: "Lettera in presente e passato prossimo" from *Paragone*, no. 256 (1971). Florence: G.C. Sansoni Editore. By permission of the publisher.

LORETTA MERENDA: "Cronaca" from *Versi d'amore* ed. by G. M. Loperfido. Venice: Corbo e Fiore Editore, 1982. By permission of the publisher.

NEGRI, ADA: "Sfida" from her volume *Poesie*. Milan: Arnoldo Mondadori Editore, 1948. By permission of A. Casella.

GIULIA NICCOLAI: "GN Is Happy" and "Dall'esterno il motivo adeguato" from her volume *Harry's Bar e altre poesie 1969–1980*. Milan: Giangiacomo Feltrinelli Editore, 1981. By permission of the publisher.

ROSSANA OMBRES: "Notturno" from her volume *Bestiario d'amore*. Milan: Rizzoli Editore, 1974. By permission of Agenzia Letteraria Internazionale, Milan.

PIERA OPPEZZO: "pianissimo" from *Versi d'amore* ed. by G. M. Loperfido. Venice: Corbo e Fiore Editore, 1982. By permission of the poet and the publisher.

AMELIA ROSSELLI: "Lo sdrucciolo cuore che in me è ribelle" and "Mio angelo, io non seppi mai quale angelo" from her volume *Documento*. Milan: Garzanti Editore, 1976. By permission of the poet and the publisher. "On Fatherish Men" from her volume *Primi scritti 1952–1963*. Milan: Guanda Editore, 1980. By permission of the poet.

GABRIELLA SICA: "Il giuramento" from *Versi d'amore* ed. by G. M. Loperfido. Venice: Corbo e Fiore Editore, 1982. By permission of the poet and the publisher.

MARIA LUISA SPAZIANI: "Per rientrare in me, per accettare" from her volume *L'occhio del ciclone*. Milan: Arnoldo Mondadori Editore, 1970. "Preghiera pagana" from her volume *Poesie*. Milan: Arnoldo Mondadori Editore, 1979. Both by permission of the publisher.

IDA VALLERUGO: "Dobbiamo liberarci oggi" from her volume *Interrogatorio*. Florence: Quaderni di Colletivo R, 1972. By permission of the publisher.

The Feminist Press at The City University of New York offers alternatives in education and in literature. Founded in 1970, this non-profit, tax-exempt educational and publishing organization works to eliminate sexual stereotypes in books and schools and to provide literature with a broad vision of human potential. The publishing program includes reprints of important works by women, feminist biographies of women, and nonsexist children's books. Curricular materials, bibliographies, directories, and a quarterly journal provide information and support for students and teachers of women's studies. In-service projects help to transform teaching methods and curricula. Through publications and projects, The Feminist Press contributes to the rediscovery of the history of women and the emergence of a more humane society.

FEMINIST CLASSICS FROM THE FEMINIST PRESS

Antoinette Brown Blackwell: A Biography, by Elizabeth Cazden. $19.95 cloth, $9.95 paper.

Between Mothers and Daughters: Stories Across a Generation. Edited by Susan Koppelman. $8.95 paper.

Brown Girl, Brownstones, a novel by Paule Marshall. Afterword by Mary Helen Washington. $8.95 paper.

Call Home the Heart, a novel of the thirties, by Fielding Burke. Introduction by Alice Kessler-Harris and Paul Lauter and afterwords by Sylvia J. Cook and Anna W. Shannon. $8.95 paper.

Cassandra, by Florence Nightingale. Introduction by Myra Stark. Epilogue by Cynthia Macdonald. $3.50 paper.

The Changelings, a novel by Jo Sinclair. Afterwords by Nellie McKay; and by Johnnetta B. Cole and Elizabeth H. Oakes; biographical note by Elisabeth Sandberg. $8.95 paper.

The Convert, a novel by Elizabeth Robins. Introduction by Jane Marcus. $6.95 paper.

Daughter of Earth, a novel by Agnes Smedley. Afterword by Paul Lauter. $7.95 paper.

A Day at a Time: The Diary Literature of American Women from 1764 to the Present, edited and with an introduction by Margo Culley. $29.95 cloth, $12.95 paper.

The Defiant Muse: French Feminist Poems from the Middle Ages to the Present, a bilingual anthology edited and with an introduction by Domna C. Stanton. $29.95 cloth, $11.95 paper.

The Defiant Muse: German Feminist Poems from the Middle Ages to the Present, a bilingual anthology edited and with an introduction by Susan L. Cocalis. $29.95 cloth, $11.95 paper.

The Defiant Muse: Hispanic Feminist Poems from the Middle Ages to the Present, a bilingual anthology edited and with an introduction by Angel Flores and Kate Flores. $29.95 cloth, $11.95 paper.

The Defiant Muse: Italian Feminist Poems from the Middle Ages to the Present, a bilingual anthology edited by Beverly Allen, Muriel Kittel, and Keala Jane Jewell, and with an introduction by Beverly Allen. $29.95 cloth, $11.95 paper.

The Female Spectator, edited by Mary R. Mahl and Helene Koon. $8.95 paper.

Guardian Angel and Other Stories, by Margery Latimer. Afterwords by Nancy Loughridge, Meridel Le Sueur, and Louis Kampf. $8.95 paper.

I Love Myself When I Am Laughing . . . And Then Again When I Am Looking Mean and Impressive, by Zora Neale Hurston. Edited by Alice Walker with an introduction by Mary Helen Washington. $9.95 paper.

Käthe Kollwitz: Woman and Artist, by Martha Kearns. $7.95 paper.

Life in the Iron Mills and Other Stories, by Rebecca Harding Davis. Biographical interpretation by Tillie Olsen. $7.95 paper.

The Living Is Easy, a novel by Dorothy West. Afterword by Adelaide M. Cromwell. $8.95 paper.

Mother to Daughter, Daughter to Mother: A Daybook and Reader, selected and shaped by Tillie Olsen. $9.95 paper.

The Other Woman: Stories of Two Women and a Man. Edited by Susan Koppelman. $8.95 paper.

Portraits of Chinese Women in Revolution, by Agnes Smedley. Edited with an introduction by Jan MacKinnon and Steve MacKinnon and an afterword by Florence Howe. $5.95 paper.

Reena and Other Stories, selected short stories by Paule Marshall. $8.95 paper.

Ripening: Selected Work, 1927–1980, by Meridel Le Sueur. Edited with an introduction by Elaine Hedges. $8.95 paper.

OTHER TITLES FROM THE FEMINIST PRESS

All The Women Are White, All The Blacks Are Men, But Some of Us Are Brave: Black Women's Studies. Edited by Gloria T. Hull, Patricia Bell Scott, and Barbara Smith. $12.95.

Black Foremothers: Three Lives, by Dorothy Sterling. $8.95 paper.

Complaints and Disorders: The Sexual Politics of Sickness, by Barbara Ehrenreich and Deirdre English. $3.95 paper.

The Cross-Cultural Study of Women. Edited by Margot I. Duley and Mary I. Edwards. $29.95 cloth, $12.95 paper.

Feminist Resources for Schools and Colleges: A Guide to Curricular Materials, 3rd edition. Compiled and edited by Anne Chapman. $12.95 paper.

Household and Kin: Families in Flux, by Amy Swerdlow et al. $8.95 paper.

How to Get Money for Research, by Mary Rubin and the Business and Professional Women's Foundation. Foreword by Mariam Chamberlain. $6.95 paper.

In Her Own Image: Women Working in the Arts. Edited with an introduction by Elaine Hedges and Ingrid Wendt. $9.95 paper.

Integrating Women's Studies into the Curriculum: A Guide and Bibliography, by Betty Schmitz. $9.95 paper.

Las Mujeres: Conversations from a Hispanic Community, by Nan Elsasser, Kyle MacKenzie, and Yvonne Tixier y Vigil. $8.95 paper.

Lesbian Studies: Present and Future. Edited by Margaret Cruikshank. $9.95 paper.

Moving the Mountain: Women Working for Social Change, by Ellen Cantarow with Susan Gushee O'Malley and Sharon Hartman Strom. $8.95 paper.

Out of the Bleachers: Writings on Women and Sport. Edited with an introduction by Stephanie L. Twin. $9.95 paper.

Reconstructing American Literature: Courses, Syllabi, Issues. Edited by Paul Lauter. $10.95 paper.

Salt of the Earth, screenplay by Michael Wilson with historical commentary by Deborah Silverton Rosenfelt. $5.95 paper.

Witches, Midwives, and Nurses: A History of Women Healers, by Barbara Ehrenreich and Deirdre English. $3.95 paper.

With These Hands: Women Working on the Land. Edited with an introduction by Joan M. Jensen. $9.95 paper.

Woman's "True" Profession: Voices from the History of Teaching. Edited with an introduction by Nancy Hoffman. $9.95 paper.

Women Have Always Worked: A Historical Overview, by Alice Kessler-Harris. $8.95 paper.

Women Working: An Anthology of Stories and Poems. Edited and with an introduction by Nancy Hoffman and Florence Howe. $8.95 paper.

For free catalog, write to The Feminist Press at The City University of New York, 311 East 94 Street, New York, N.Y. 10128. Send individual book orders to The Feminist Press, P.O. Box 1654, Hagerstown, MD 21741. Include $1.75 postage and handling for one book and 75¢ for each additional book. To order using MasterCard or Visa, call: (800) 638-3030.